Better Homes and Gardens®

celebrate the SEASON

1999

Better Homes and Gardens® Books
Des Moines, Iowa

Better Homes and Gardens® Books
An imprint of Meredith® Books

Celebrate the Season 1999
Editor: Vicki L. Ingham
Art Director / Graphic Designer: Marisa Dirks
Food Editor: Kristi Fuller
Assistant Food Editor: Chuck Smothermon
Contributing Editors: Paula Marshall, Joyce Trollope
Contributing Writers: Laura H. Collins, Jennifer Crutcher Wilkinson
Copy Chief: Catherine Hamrick
Copy and Production Editor: Terri Fredrickson
Contributing Copy Editor: Jay Lamar
Contributing Proofreaders: Nancy Dietz, Fran Gardner, Debra Morris Smith
Electronic Production Coordinator: Paula Forest
Editorial and Design Assistants: Kaye Chabot, Judy Bailey, Mary Lee Gavin, Karen Schirm
Test Kitchen Director: Sharon Stilwell
Production Director: Douglas M. Johnston
Production Manager: Pam Kvitne
Assistant Prepress Manager: Marjorie J. Schenkelberg

Meredith® Books
Editor in Chief: James D. Blume
Design Director: Matt Strelecki
Managing Editor: Gregory H. Kayko
Executive Shelter Editor: Denise L. Caringer

Director, Sales & Marketing, Retail: Michael A. Peterson
Director, Sales & Marketing, Special Markets: Rita McMullen
Director, Sales & Marketing, Home & Garden Center Channel: Ray Wolf
Director, Operations: George A. Susral

Vice President, General Manager: Jamie L. Martin

Better Homes and Gardens® Magazine
Editor in Chief: Jean LemMon
Executive Interior Design Editor: Sandra S. Soria
Executive Food Editor: Nancy Byal

Meredith Publishing Group
President, Publishing Group: Christopher M. Little
Vice President, Consumer Marketing & Development: Hal Oringer

Meredith Corporation
Chairman and Chief Executive Officer: William T. Kerr

Chairman of the Executive Committee: E. T. Meredith III

All of us at Better Homes and Gardens® Books are dedicated to providing you with information and ideas to enhance your home. We welcome your comments and suggestions. Write to us at: Better Homes and Gardens® Books, Shelter Editorial Department, 1716 Locust St., Des Moines, IA 50309-3023. Or visit our website at www.bhg.com.

If you would like to order additional copies of this book, call 800/439-7159.

Cover photograph: King Au

Our seal assures you that every recipe in *Celebrate the Season* has been tested in the Better Homes and Gardens® Test Kitchen. This means that each recipe is practical and reliable and meets our high standards of taste appeal. We guarantee your satisfaction with this book for as long as you own it.

time...

there's never enough of it, especially during the holidays. Because time is so precious, it's one of the best gifts you can give to others and to yourself. This year, think about your holiday "to-do" list as little gifts of time to bestow on family and friends. Look at decorating as a form of creative expression, and you'll give yourself a double gift: the pleasure of the process as well as enjoyment of the results. The ideas in this book can get you started and help you indulge your imagination. Time spent with family and friends is its own reward. Whether you plan a quiet evening at home, a buffet for a crowd, or a noisy salute to the New Year, you'll find recipes to suit the occasion in this year's book. Since time *is* such a valuable commodity, be sure to check the "In a Twinkling" pages for quick decorating and gift ideas. Above all, relax and give yourself time to enjoy the season.

Vicki Ingham

— Vicki Ingham, Editor

You're invited to an

Open House

Ann and Dave Greene
8224 Long Ridge Road

Cocktails and buffet supper
7:00 p.m.

*Come share
the spirit of the season
with us!*

Moss Frame

■ In this season of festivity, welcome friends to your home with a mossy rectangular wreath on your door. To make it, tape a purchased 11x14-inch picture mat inside an 11x14-inch plain wood frame. Center and tape an 8x10-inch mat over the opening in the 11x14 mat. Cover the mats and frame with brown paper, securing it with masking tape. Use hotmelt adhesive to attach pads of moss to the paper, covering the entire frame. (Ask your florist to order fresh mood moss for you, or use dried bun moss. The mood moss holds its green color when it dries.) Add a bow and pinecones as desired.

table *of* contents

setting the stage

gathering together

giving from the heart

kids' stuff

In a Twinkling
Easy-to-use ideas for the holidays

What's your holiday-decorating personality? Are you cozily traditional, happily putting up the same decorations in the same places every year? Or are you experimental, always trying out a new look? Do you like spare and subtle decorations that don't clutter a room? Or do you feel cheated if every room doesn't wear at least a few pieces of holiday finery? Whether you're of the "less is more" school of thought or the "more is always better" group, you'll find ideas and decorations to inspire you on the following pages. Accessories you make yourself infuse rooms with holiday spirit. And don't forget to dress up the outside of your house, too. Your home is the scene for celebration—let it reflect your personal style.

6

SETTING

the STAGE

Give your Christmas decorations a new look every year by changing the ways you use or display them. Let the following ideas inspire you!

one room
three ways

If you have ornaments and decorations you cherish, but you like to do something different every year, think about new ways to use what you have. Adding one or two new unifying elements refreshes the look without breaking your budget.

On the following pages, we used the same basic collection of decorations to create two different looks. For the third year, we introduced lighter colors that still work with the basics from the previous two years. Even if you don't have decorations just like these, you can still apply the principles (see page 14 for more ideas).

Year One

If most of your ornaments are a handmade or mix-and-match collection, consider supplementing them with a group of generic ornaments. Gold snowflakes, icicles, and glass balls or teardrops in clear, white, and a favorite color (such as red or burgundy) form a backdrop for your special decorations or any themes you want to emphasize. To create a rich, romantic look in burgundy and gold, for example, add velvet poinsettias and ornaments, tassels, gold fruit, and cranberry-bead garland; crown the tree with a bouquet of gold balls and gilded fruit that can later serve as a centerpiece. (For instructions for the tree topper, see page 15.)

mantel

To decorate the mantel, use an artificial garland as a base and insert sprigs of fresh cedar, juniper, and fir. Tuck in individual velvet poinsettias. You can buy them by the stem at crafts stores and floral-supply shops, or look for a "bush" that includes nine or 10 individual blooms. Use green floral wire to secure tasseled drapery cording to the greenery, arranging the cording and tassels to swag across the fireplace in asymmetrical loops as shown.

To carry the treatment above the mantel, insert poinsettias into a fresh wreath and wire drapery cording to it as well. Loop the cording across the wreath so the tassels hang on each side at different levels. Link the mantel visually to the wreath with burgundy candles of varying heights and shapes.

10

coffee table

For a coffee table, place three tall candlesticks in the center of the table. Lay branches of fresh greenery in a radiating pattern on the table (be sure the cut ends aren't dripping sap), then arrange wrapped packages on the greenery. These could be packages you intend to give; or wrap boxes of different sizes and shapes like miniature works of art and use them for decorating from year to year.

To decorate the packages, use odds and ends of ribbon and leftover artificial leaves or fruits. Cut the ribbons to fit the box, trimming the ends to points or overlapping the ends slightly. Glue a gold pinecone over the ends to suggest a button tab, or adhere artificial leaves and grapes in a symmetrical arrangement on the top.

To duplicate the tall box at the center right of the photo *above*, glue a leaf so it wraps one corner of a box, and fold ribbon over the next corner along the length of the box. Decorate the top with silk leaves, a pinecone, and twigs glued with pan-melt hotmelt adhesive. This miniature arrangement can be saved and used as a decoration or place-card holder for the table.

SHOPPING LIST

From a crafts store or floral-
supply shop:
 10-inch plastic foam ball
 30 to 40 pearl-tipped
  corsage pins
 pan-melt hotmelt
  adhesive
 2 artificial white
  magnolias with buds
 6 clusters of latex grapes
  with leaves
 2 or 3 stems of artificial
  dogwood
 7 pinecones sprayed gold
 artificial pine
 gold berry sprays
 dried-look silk
  rosebuds
From a fabric store:
 1 yard of crinkle-texture
  stretch velvet
 6 yards of drapery
  cording

4 Working around the edges of the opening, insert the clusters of grapes, curving them so they lead the eye around the ball. Tuck a gold berry spray under one of the magnolias.

window

For a window, make a hanging globe ornament; next year, it can go upside down on a large candlestick and serve as a Christmas "gazing ball."

2 From 3 yards of drapery cording, cut four equal lengths. Knot the pieces together at one end. Knot the remaining ends, then secure them to the ball at four equally spaced points around the opening by pinning them in place with corsage pins dipped in hotmelt adhesive.

here's how...

1

Center the plastic foam ball on the velvet, and pull the fabric tightly around the ball, leaving a 6-inch opening at what will be the top. Use the corsage pins to hold the velvet in place, and trim away the excess fabric around the top. Insert additional corsage pins in a diamond pattern around the ball for texture.

3

Choose one side to be the front, and insert the magnolias on each side of this area, positioning one to face up and one to face out. Nestle the flowers close to the ball's surface. At the back of the ball, insert a 16-inch-tall dogwood stem so it forms the top of an S. Position a second dogwood stem toward the front, completing the S curve.

5

Fill in around the top of the ball with pinecones, gold berries, pine sprigs, and grape leaves. Add the dried-look rosebuds evenly around the arrangement to emphasize the lines of the flower stems.

6 From the remaining drapery cord, make a two-loop bow, securing it with floral wire. Tuck it into the ball under one of the magnolias.

11

12

ONE ROOM THREE WAYS: YEAR ONE

lamp corsage

For table lamps, assemble a corsage of artificial gold berries, leaves, and dried-look silk flowers. Use wired gold cording or bend the wired stems of the flowers to form a hook to hang over the top edge of the lampshade.

to serve as a stem for assembling the corsage). Layer the wired cording bow over the ribbon bow and twist the wire tails together. Wrap the ends of the wired cording around a pencil to create curls.

Wrap the stems of the dried-look rosebuds with green floral tape, then cut the stems to staggered lengths. Tuck the dried-look rosebuds into the front of the bouquet to frame the gold rosebuds. Wrap the corsage stem with green floral tape. Bend the stems of the leaves and flowers so they radiate gracefully from the center of the corsage.

4 Fold a 10-inch length of wired gold cording in half and knot the ends. Twist the knotted ends around the corsage stem; bend the loop to form a hanger that fits over the edge of the lampshade.

here's how...

Make a six-loop bow from the wired cording and a four- to six-loop bow from the ribbon, securing the center of each with floral wire (leave wire "tails" on each

Place the gold rosebuds over the center of the bows and arrange the gold berry sprays around them. Wrap the stems and bow wires with floral tape. Add the gold leaves to the back, and wrap again with floral tape.

Year Two

A simple switching of elements produces a sumptuous display. Use the gold fruit or some of the ornaments that hung on the tree last year to decorate a fresh wreath and the mantel this year. Replace the burgundy candles with the velvet ornaments, standing them on the candlesticks, and add new ribbon—we combined a 2-inch-wide green, burgundy, and gold check with a narrower red-and-green plaid and a solid gold. Use the ribbons to make a bow for the wreath and to wind through the garland on the mantel; also make a big bow for the tree topper.

Turn the ball arrangement upside down and stand it on a tall pedestal candlestick for a hearthside or hallway accent. Shape the stems so they sweep upward and reverse the grape clusters so they droop downward. Loop the long hanging cords among the stems.

here's how...

tree

Tuck the velvet poinsettias among the tree branches and use florist's wire to attach the drapery cording and tassels so they swag from branch to branch around the tree. To make bows from smaller drapery tiebacks, fold and wire the cording into loops.

13

wreath

here's how...

For a lavish look, make two bows and insert them in the upper left quadrant of the wreath; add a long streamer separately. To attach the gold fruit that hung on the tree last year, push a length of heavy florist's wire into one end of each piece, and then push the wire into the wreath's foam base. If your wreath is on a wire base, push the wire through to the back and twist it around the wire base.

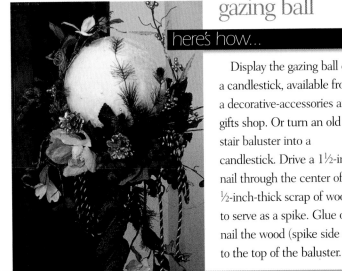

gazing ball

here's how...

Display the gazing ball on a candlestick, available from a decorative-accessories and gifts shop. Or turn an old stair baluster into a candlestick. Drive a 1½-inch nail through the center of a ½-inch-thick scrap of wood to serve as a spike. Glue or nail the wood (spike side up) to the top of the baluster.

how to have a new look every year

■ Instead of hanging all of your ornaments on your tree, display some of them as collections. Old-fashioned blown-glass figures or theme ornaments can have more impact if you pile them in a bowl or hang them on a wreath instead of dispersing them over the tree.

■ Think of candlesticks as pedestals and use them to show off special ornaments or to hold orbs of all kinds—marble spheres, large glass ornaments, or balls covered with moss, seeds, or bark. The orbs may be decorative accessories you display all year, but when you cluster them on the mantel and add greenery and holiday ribbon, they become a festive seasonal accent.

■ Shop for good-quality wire-edge holiday ribbon when it's on sale, and use it year after year—one year's double-bow tree topper becomes the next year's wreath bow. Ribbon streamers looped through the tree one year can wrap a garland on the mantel or stair the next.

■ Look for seasonal elements that can do double or triple duty: velvet poinsettias, for example, can decorate the mantel one year, the tree the next, and candlesticks or packages the following year.

■ Don't forget to embellish everyday objects with holiday touches: a corsage of artificial berries and flowers can dress up a lampshade or a framed family photo, focusing attention on them in a new way.

■ Transform your home for the holidays with holiday artwork, such as framed Santa posters or reproduction Currier and Ives winter scenes. And don't forget table runners and pillows in seasonal fabrics. A table runner can dress the dining table, a sofa table or coffee table, or even the mantel.

■ Give your tree a different look each year by adding one new unifying element. Candy canes, crocheted snowflakes, paper roses, or a single color of glass balls hung evenly over the tree ties together your collection of handmade and acquired-over-the-years ornaments while changing the overall character of the tree from year to year.

SHOPPING LIST

deep, small-necked jar
From a crafts store or
    floral-supply shop:
    18-inch-long hyacinth
        stick or slender dowel
    medium-weight
        floral wire
    pan-melt hotmelt
        adhesive
    floral tape
    assorted gilded artificial
        fruit (pear, apple, 2
        pomegranates)
    medium and small
        gold glass balls
    pinecones sprayed gold
    large gilded artificial
        rose and rosebuds
    several stems of
        artificial pine
    artificial grape leaves
        and rose leaves,
        sprayed gold
    gold berry sprays
    2 gold artificial fruit sprays
    silver poppy pods

To assemble the arrangement, insert the fruits into the small-necked jar to form a pyramid shape. Place the open rose at the center and insert a few pinecones and balls to emphasize the shape of the arrangement.

5 Assemble a "cascade" or long, thin bouquet using a stem of rosebuds as the backbone. Arrange pinecones, berry sprays, fruit sprays, and silver poppy pods along the stem, staggering their placement. Wire the stems together, then wrap with floral tape. Bend the wrapped stems and insert the cascade into the jar at the base of the arrangement.

6 Fill out the arrangement with pine and the remaining glass balls, pinecones, and grape leaves. Carefully lift the

coffee table

Move last year's tree topper to the coffee table and stand it in a tall glass vase to serve as a centerpiece. Arrange burgundy and green candles around it and "drizzle" the cranberry-bead garland among the candlesticks for a graceful line.

here's how...

1 Dip one end of a piece of floral wire into pan-melt hotmelt adhesive, then push it into one end of each piece of artificial fruit. Starting close to the fruit, wrap the wire with floral tape. Set aside.

Remove the caps from the small and medium glass balls. To make a stem for each ball, fold an 18-inch-long piece of floral wire in half, dip the fold in hotmelt

adhesive, and insert the fold into the opening of the ball. (You may need to dip the fold into the adhesive several times, letting the glue harden between dips, to build up enough glue to fill the opening of the ball.) After the glue dries, wrap the ball's neck and the wire stem with floral tape. Set aside.

3 To attach a stem to each pinecone, make a small hole in the base of the pinecone with an ice pick or a drill, dip a piece of floral wire into hotmelt adhesive, and push the glued end into the hole. Or wrap wire around the base of the pinecone, working it under the lowest open scales; twist the wire ends tightly at the base of the cone. Wrap the wire with floral tape.

arrangement out of the jar and wrap the stems together tightly with floral wire.

7 Carefully push the hyacinth stick down into the center of the arrangement until it's hidden. Wrap the stems and stick with wire and cover with floral tape.

Year Three

tree

Shift to a lighter, more contemporary look with sage, verdigris, and creamy white elements. On the coffee table, use the velvet poinsettias to make corsages for tall candlesticks (see the instructions on page 17). Use cotton-covered floral wire to attach tassels to candlesticks, too. Center a fresh or artificial wreath on the table and arrange the candlesticks inside and around the outside of the wreath. Decorate the wreath's face with gold fruit, frosted-glass ornaments, and ribbons that match the tree topper.

Garland the tree with swaths of cheesecloth (we used 8 yards for a 6-foot tree) and long stems of variegated artificial ivy. To crinkle the cheesecloth, simply wet it and let it dry. Gather up the cheesecloth at intervals with clusters of verdigris-colored artificial grapes, apples, and pears.

For the top of the tree, layer ribbon streamers of different lengths and widths and wire them to a piece of silk ivy. Center and wire a gold fruit spray over the streamers.

SHOPPING LIST:
2 velvet poinsettias
3 stems of artificial pine
6 to 10 inches long
a stem of gold rose leaves
floral wire
floral tape
1 yard of gold
wired cording

poinsettia corsages

here's how...

1 Layer the pine stems behind the poinsettias, bending the pine to suggest a fan shape behind the poinsettias.

2 Tuck the gold rose leaves behind the pine, then wire all stems together tightly.

3 Wrap the wired stems with floral tape so the wire won't scratch your candlestick. Continue wrapping all the way down the stems. To attach the corsage, bend the wrapped stems around the candlestick just below the candle cup. Clip off any excess stem.

sofa table

here's how...

For the sofa table, cut the long stem off the tree topper from Year One, and stand it on a runner to serve as a mini-tree. Add streamers of ribbon from Year Two, and wind artificial variegated ivy around the stems of the candlestick lamps. Wire a tassel to the top of each lamp using cotton-covered floral wire.

mantel

here's how...

Hang a Christmas print or poster instead of a wreath, and lay lengths of fresh or artificial holly and ivy along the frame's top edge. For a clean, architectural look on the mantel, drape it with a table runner or mantel scarf and arrange a collection of candles and orbs on mismatched candlesticks. Use spheres of various textures and materials—large ornaments, round candles, silver wire-mesh orbs, and balls covered with moss, bay leaves, grasses, or silver studs—and rest them on the mantel as well as atop candlesticks. Add sparkle and interest with packages wrapped in copper and gold tissue paper. Tuck stems of fresh greenery among the candlesticks and packages to give them a soft "base."

No room for lavish decorations?
Choose a focal point and concentrate your efforts there.

Whether you live in an efficiency apartment or a quaint but crowded bungalow, you may find yourself space-challenged for the holidays. That doesn't need to prevent you from creating a festive atmosphere in your already cozy home. The secret is to choose one area, preferably a highly visible one, and focus your decorations in that spot.

bring the holidays in focus

■ If you don't have a fireplace, give your living area a focal point by turning the coffee table or an old trunk into a surface for decorating. A tiny tree, either live or artificial, can provide the center of interest; arrange wrapped packages, votive candles, and a few old toys around it to set a holiday mood.

■ Other surfaces that can be a stage for festive displays include the dining or breakfast table, the top of a tall chest of drawers, or an armoire, sideboard, or sofa table.

■ If the best thing about your apartment or loft is the view, decorate the windows by swagging them with greenery and lights, hanging ornaments from tension rods inserted in the window frames, or arranging candles and greenery on the window sills (see pages 22–23 for more ideas).

The Mantel

❧ If you have a fireplace, the mantel is a natural place for the eye to rest. Here a wreath hangs in the center of a year-round display of transferware. If you have a painting over the mantel, tuck evergreen branches behind the painting and let their weight hold them in place along the top of the frame.

To soften the mantel, layer it with fabric. A crisp white dresser scarf brings a clean, fresh look to a crowded room. (If you like a weightier look, use a velvet or damask table runner or several yards of fabric draped along the shelf.) For a family Christmas theme, assemble framed photos along the mantel; use a variety of frame sizes and alternate horizontal and vertical formats to keep the eye moving along the mantel. Overlap some of the frames and rest ornaments and evergreens among the photos to create depth. Add a pair of candlesticks for height, and dress them up with bows and greenery.

quick ideas for

small spaces

A Side Table

꿈 You don't have to host a sit-down dinner to enjoy the company of friends during the holidays. Invite them over for coffee and dessert, and let the food and accoutrements set a festive mood with color: red and white candy, napkins, and cups play on the red-and-white theme of the coffeepot and candles here.

Arrange the items as you would accessories, paying attention to varying heights and shapes, so your presentation is pleasing to look at as well as practical for serving. A pie server is a good way to add height; this one is filled with apples and hydrangeas to continue the red and white theme. (Look for pie servers in the kitchen department of home furnishings stores and in home decorating catalogs.)

The Chandelier

꿈 If there's not a free surface to be found, look up for a decorating spot. Chandeliers offer sparkling opportunities for creating a festive mood in the room. Wire sprigs of fresh greenery to the arms of the fixture and tie bows under each light. Hang crystal and teardrop ornaments from the arms, suspending them at different levels to help lead your eye upward to the chandelier.

Screen your view of the outdoors with an indoor forest of skinny Christmas trees. Anchor the trees in wet sand in galvanized buckets, and add watering cans for a garden theme.

In a Twinkling: Windows

◄ Frame the window from inside with miniature lights. Run a strand of lights along the sill and top of the sash, securing it with small pieces of masking tape. Suspend a lighted tree-topper ornament from the sash (or pop a specialty add-on ornament onto one of the miniature lights—see page 30 for more information). Hide the wires with greenery.

◀ Let it snow—indoors! Dress up a window with a lacy table skirt for a quick valance and hang paper snowflakes from the curtain rod with ribbon.

◀ Arrange red and green bottles along the top of a window sash where they can catch the light and filter your view with Christmas color.

▲ Bring a view into focus with a lightweight wreath of artificial eucalyptus. Wire several stems together in a circle to make the wreath and hang it in front of the window with clear monofilament.

▲ Accent windows with swags of artificial eucalyptus and silk or dried red flowers. Bundle stems of eucalyptus, red twigs, dyed-red baby's breath, and bear grass into a small swag; assemble red yarrow into another smaller bouquet and wire it over the swag's stem ends. Tie a bow over the joining and bend one eucalyptus branch to form a hanger to hook over the curtain rod.

Welcome fall with arrangements that take advantage of the season's harvest. Use deep green and cream fruits instead of yellow and orange, and they'll carry over to Christmas.

autumn
in the air

Winter squash and miniature pumpkins and gourds are readily available at farmers' markets and grocery stores in the fall. Look for new varieties, such as white pumpkins, to give a fresh look to traditional decorations. Choose deep-green winter squash and creamy gourds as the basis of your autumn arrangements; for Christmas, simply add evergreens and red fruit, such as pomegranates, red pears, or apples.

Mini Pumpkin Topiary

here's how...

1

Cut two 2-inch pieces of wire from a coat hanger.

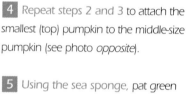

2

Insert one end of one piece of wire into or beside the stem of the largest miniature pumpkin. Using the hot-glue gun, place a drop of hotmelt adhesive where the wire enters the fruit.

3

Insert the other end of the wire into the bottom of the middle-size pumpkin.

4 Repeat steps 2 and 3 to attach the smallest (top) pumpkin to the middle-size pumpkin (see photo *opposite*).

5 Using the sea sponge, pat green paint onto the terra-cotta pot, allowing the clay color of the pot to show through. (Instead of a sea sponge, you can use a cellulose sponge; tear away pieces from the surface to roughen it, then use it to pat paint onto the pot.)

6

Fill the terra-cotta pot with craft foam, almost to the top. Pin a collar of leaves to the foam with U pins. Insert a short piece of coat-hanger wire into the bottom of the lowest pumpkin, then push the other end into the crafts foam. Tie raffia around the pot's rim, and glue sprigs of bittersweet to the raffia.

3 miniature
    pumpkins in
    graduated sizes
wire coat hanger
wire clippers
hot-glue gun
    and glue sticks
small terra-cotta pot
green acrylic paint
sea sponge or
    cellulose sponge
crafts foam
U pins
silk or fresh
    autumn leaves
bittersweet, raffia

Pomegranate and Hydrangea Wreath

SHOPPING LIST:

newspaper and
plastic to cover
work surface
wire coat hanger
pomegranates
hydrangeas

here's how...

1 Protect the work surface with layers of newspaper, covered with plastic.

2 Untwist the coat hanger at the base of the hook. Shape the wire into a circle, then push pomegranates onto it. Thread the wire through the side of the fruit so the blossom end faces out. Add fruit until the circle is filled up to the base of the hook.

3 Retwist the coat-hanger wire at the base of the hook.

4 Hang the wreath by the hook over the plastic-protected work surface, and let the juices drain.

5 After the pomegranates have drained, tuck hydrangea blossoms between the fruits. (You may want to secure the flowers with hotmelt adhesive.) Use the coat-hanger hook to hang the wreath.

■ *Bridge the holidays from Thanksgiving to Christmas with this wreath.*

27

Centerpiece

➥ To achieve impact with a centerpiece like this, be bold: instead of an ordinary grapevine wreath for the base, look for heavy ones made of thick, gnarled vines and nest two to form a bowl. Instead of a lone pillar candle for the center, choose a large hurricane lamp and candleholder. And rather than placing just a few fruits around the wreath, pile generous amounts of fruits in a variety of shapes, sizes, and colors. This centerpiece includes red and yellow pears, apples, kumquats, tangerines, and limes. If you have crab apple trees or fall-fruiting shrubs, cut some branches to add to the display.

28

Winter Squash Vase

SHOPPING LIST

large Hubbard
    squash
utility knife
fresh mums or
    other fall flowers
bittersweet
several yards of
    3-inch-wide
    organdy ribbon

Set the squash on its side to find a stable resting position. Use a knife to cut a 2-inch-square plug out of the top. It isn't necessary to scoop out the insides, but do pour a little water into the hole.

29

Cut the mum stems to 10 to 12 inches in length. Center the ribbon under the flower heads, then wrap it around and down the stems, stopping about 2 inches from the bottom. Tie the ribbon in a knot to secure it at this point.

Insert the flower stems in the 2-inch hole, securing them in the squash's flesh. Tie the ribbon in a bow. Tuck sprigs and branches of bittersweet into the squash vase around the base of the flowers.

Lighting options abound. Now you can make as much of a personal statement with lights as you do with ornaments.

lighting up the night

Indoors

Clear or multicolored, miniature or standard—those used to be about your only choices for holiday lights. Bubble lights were the most adventuresome option you could readily find, and even those eventually fell out of favor. But manufacturers have seen the light. Choose from a variety of bulb covers and color palettes—or mix and match to brighten Christmas trees, mantels, and stairways, or to illuminate the outside of your house.

Bulb Covers—Ornament-style bulb covers snap over miniature bulbs, clipping to tree branches for stability. Scatter a few around the tree for eye-catching results.

A strand or two of snowballs or icicles add an "ahhhh" factor to mantels or stairways. These lights are often oversized, making them overwhelming on a tree, so use them judiciously.

Colors—Which white would you like: clear, frosted, or pearlized? Each gives a different glow. You'll find these whites alone on strands or mixed in with other colors.

If you prefer color, use full strands of a single jewel-toned hue for dramatic effect. Cool teal blues or warm golden yellows are just two of many new colors available. Or choose a multicolor strand. The standard four-color spectrum has a cozily old-fashioned look, or you can opt for more contemporary, vibrant colors that follow a theme— blue, teal, and green, for example. You'll also find strands with a frosty white or clear bulb in the color sequence to accent the colored bulbs.

▲ String a strand of snowball lights around a door, along a mantel, or down a banister for a glittering display reminiscent of a winter's day. Remember, a little goes a long way with big bulbs like this. On a tree, use just a couple of strands in a sweeping overlay—like a scant garland— to supplement your standard lights.

◀ Red, clear, and white lights create a candy-cane look that's charming wherever they're used. Simple combinations of miniature bulbs like this create a sweet scene that blends neatly into the decoration of any tree.

30

lighting
standards

■ More color and style options aren't the only improvements in lighting; new strands are designed to be safer, too. In order to receive the Underwriters Laboratories' (UL) seal of approval, all lights produced after January 1, 1997, have to meet these new standards.

■ The insulation around the wires is thicker to reduce the risk of exposing live wires.

■ Wires are tested to ensure they have adequate flex so they'll hold up for installation and storage.

■ Bulbs are now cooler, so less likely to cause burns.

■ Every strand comes with two replacement bulbs.

■ Tips for use, care, inspection, and storage also are included with every strand of lights.

To make sure the bulbs you buy meet the new standards, look for a mark noting UL588-17th edition on the box or on a tag attached to the strand. The new standard applies to lights rated for indoor or outdoor use.

▶

Elegant jewel tones in this "renaissance"-theme light strand create a deep, rich look. Choose a color scheme that sets the mood you're after, especially for a theme tree.

Outdoors

〰 Whatever style of outdoor lighting you choose, installing it can be a snap with the new styles of clips and stakes.

Getting a strand of outdoor lights evenly spaced and facing the same direction used to be quite an accomplishment. As much as outdoor lights are a beauty to behold, they can be a beast to install—twisting this way, not turning that way—and you're trying to tame this unwieldy tangle while standing on a ladder on a chilly December day.

A little Yankee ingenuity has come to the rescue. New styles of clips that attach to the gutter or roof shingles make it easier to space bulbs evenly along the roofline and allow you to easily direct the lights (see *page 33*).

Made of a sturdy plastic, the clips snap together and into place with ease. And the clips come in styles suited for standard or miniature lights. (For source information, see page 158.)

32

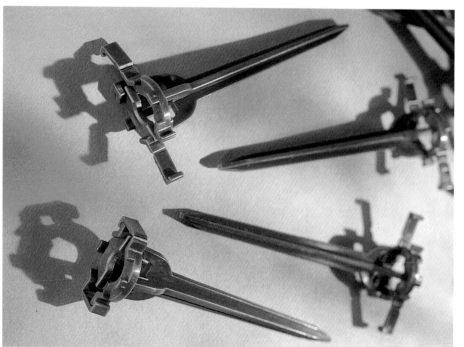

◀ Light the path to your door with a strand of standard or mini lights and these light stakes. Simply push the stakes into the ground, slip in the lights, and close the plastic hinges around both sides of the cord to hold the lights in place. Swish some snow or moss between the lights to cover the exposed cord. (Tip: If the ground is frozen, use an old screwdriver and hammer to create a starter hole.)

before you start

■ Do the math. Measure the distance to cover, and figure out how many lights and clips are needed. Chances are the length of the strands won't match the total length required and you'll need to do some adjusting. For a brighter display, place clips closer together, or run two alternating strands.

■ Test your lights. Plug in each strand ahead of time to be sure each bulb lights up and that the sockets and cords are solid. Replace strands with brittle cords or cracked or loose sockets.

■ Check the connections. Be sure the connections between strands are compatible and the extension cord easily reaches the plug. Check the manufacturer's recommendations for the maximum number of strands to connect to each other. You may need to use a second extension cord.

■ Measure carefully. If you're using special spacing between lights, cut a piece of cardboard or a strip of wood to the exact length. Use it to measure the space between clips.

◄ As icicle lights travel along the outlines of your house, they may need to attach to both gutters and shingles. These universal clips attach firmly to either surface, making installation a breeze.

33

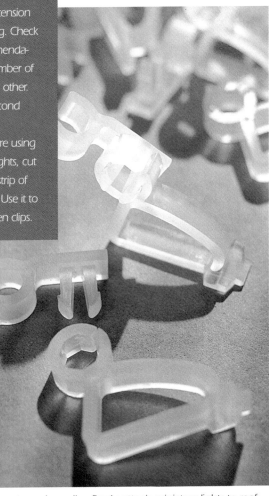

▲ These two-piece clips firmly attach miniature lights to roof shingles. The adjustable base holder allows you to direct the lights to the angle that best illuminates your house.

▲ Sometimes simplest is best. For straightforward, straight-line house lighting situations, a good gutter clip may be all that is needed. Choose one like this that fastens firmly to the gutter and snugly secures the cord. Made of thick but flexible plastic, clips like these are designed to withstand years of cold weather and sunlight without becoming brittle.

Most of your neighbors see only the outside of your house—so what better way to spread your holiday spirit than with outdoor decorations? Let these ideas inspire you.

decorating the
great outdoors

Lights, luminarias, and nearly lifesize wooden cutouts (such as reindeer and angels) are popular, but don't limit yourself to these. Outdoor decorations give you a chance to express your personality. Bears on a porch swing or geese dressed for a party will make passersby smile; vine balls and fresh evergreens blend elegantly into the landscape for a more subtle look.

winter gazing ball

Put your empty birdbath to work for the holidays. Rest a fresh wreath on the rim of the bowl, and place a vine ball in the center. To add some sparkle, thread a strand of battery-operated tiny white lights into the ball through one of the openings. Use green floral wire to attach the light cord to the vines around the ball; otherwise all the lights will fall to the bottom.

welcoming committee

If your porch is protected from the weather, create a holiday vignette with stuffed bears, colorful blankets, skis, sleds, and greenery.

36

Vine-Ball Accents

 Swag a balcony or deck railing with purchased evergreen garland, and accent each swag with a trio of vine balls. Look for the balls in holiday catalogs and garden shops. Use sturdy crafts wire to attach two vine balls to the deck railing, then wire the third ball to the first two.

Snowflake Lantern

SHOPPING LIST:
tissue paper or
tracing paper
adhesive tape
lantern with glass
panels
Delta CeramDecor
paint: silver
paintbrush

Light the way to your front door with a snowflake-painted lantern. Available from chain home furnishings stores, the lantern holds a pillar candle—you add the snowflakes with paint. Stand the lantern in the center of a fresh wreath on a table on your patio or deck, or let it hang from a lantern hook. (The heat from the candle will make the top of the lantern very hot, so use caution when opening the door.)

1 Draw a stick-figure snowflake onto a scrap of tissue paper or tracing paper.

2 Refer to the photograph for placement and tape the snowflake pattern to the inside of the glass.

3 Paint the snowflake on the outside of the glass with silver paint. Reposition the snowflake pattern, and paint a complete or partial snowflake. Continue painting snowflakes on the glass panels until the composition is completed. Allow the paint to dry.

Garden Geese

Those rusted-metal geese that adorn your garden year-round are ready to party for the holidays. Perk them up with appropriate party clothes—a child's red-plaid necktie, a Santa cap intended for a teddy bear, a little girl's holiday hair bow, and strands of sparkly plastic Mardi Gras beads dress this foursome.

garden urn with an
8-inch-diameter
opening
about 30 lemons
medium-weight
florist's wire
lemon leaves

lemon
topiary

This pyramid of lemons in a classic garden urn brings a sophisticated holiday look to a mantel, hearth, or hall table—and it's surprisingly easy to make. If you don't happen to have an old cast-iron garden urn, look for a plaster reproduction in home-decorating shops and crafts stores.

38

here's how...

1 Thread eight lemons onto a length of wire, pushing the wire through each lemon near one end. Shape the wire into a ring to fit the opening of the urn and twist the wire ends together.

2 Make a second ring the same size and a third ring that's slightly smaller. Stack the three rings on the urn as shown.

3 Thread four or five lemons onto wire to make a smaller ring, and stack this ring on top of the pyramid. Finish with a single lemon on top.

4 Tuck lemon leaves (also called salal, available from a florist) between the fruits.

SHOPPING LIST

tree limb
old weathered
    board or plank
nails
sheet moss or
    sphagnum moss
9 copper pipe
    end-caps
vise grips or clamp
center punch or awl
variable-speed electric
    drill and twist bit
screws
9 candles

woodland
menorah

2 Secure the caps, one at a time, to your work surface with a vise or clamp. Use the center punch to mark the position of the screw hole in the center of the cap, then drill a hole through the copper cap.

3

Mark the placement of the candle cups on the tree limb, spacing them evenly along the top of the limb. The cup for the ninth candle, which is used to light the others, should be higher, lower, or out of line with the other eight candles. Make a pilot hole for each screw, using the drill or an awl. Screw the candle cups in place.

4 Cover the board and parts of the log with sphagnum moss.

❧ A fallen tree limb that's about 4 or 5 inches in diameter can serve as a natural base for a rustic menorah.

here's how...

1

Working from the underside, nail the board or plank to the tree limb to make a level base.

◀ Dress up family photos with holiday corsages. Assemble miniature versions of the lampshade corsages shown on *page 12*. Or simply wire together a few sprigs of greenery and berries and bend the wire to form a hook to hang over the frame's edge.

In a Twinkling:Details

▶

Bring a bit of Christmas to any spot—a table in the entry, beside the sink in the powder room, a side table or bookcase in the den—with a mini-tree made by layering fresh fir tips on a stacked candy dish. Add a ribbon and some sprigs of holly for color.

For a festive accent at your windows, replace your everyday curtain tiebacks with yards of ribbon. Use three to five different widths of ribbon, and mix satin, grosgrain, and organdy for a rich effect. Attach jingle bells to the ribbon ends by threading the ribbon through the top of the bell and knotting it. To attach pinecones, wrap floral wire around the bottom scales of the pinecone and twist the wire ends to form a loop. Knot the ribbon through the loop.

41

Add a merry touch to every room with holiday light-switch covers. Buy inexpensive plastic covers at the hardware store. Cut holiday gift wrap about an inch larger all around and glue it to the cover with a mixture of equal parts thick white crafts glue and water. Fold the excess paper to the back and glue it in place. From the back, cut an X across the switch opening and glue the tabs to the back of the cover *(above left)*, then coat the front with two or three coats of the glue mixture. Check hardware stores for clear acrylic cover kits *(left)* for an even easier alternative.

Extend a cheerful holiday welcome with a wreath that reflects your own personal style. Outdoor wreaths should be sturdy and weighty looking. Indoors, they can be more delicate.

wreaths to *welcome* the season

Making the full, traditional style of wreaths shown on these pages is easy if you begin with a purchased grapevine base and glue or wire clusters of leaves to it. Or, for an even faster alternative, use a fresh or artificial fir wreath as a base and insert lemon leaves from the florist or magnolia from your yard for contrasting texture. To make lightweight wreaths to hang indoors, try the holly and ivy wreath or the kumquat ring on *page 45*; both start with a metal ring like you'd use for macramé.

Citrus Wreath
here's how...

1 Clip the lemon leaves into 8- to 10-inch-long branches. Push the branches into the grapevine wreath, working around the wreath so all the stem ends point in the same direction.

2 Wrap floral wire around the lower scales of each pinecone, twisting the wire ends together to form a tail.

3 To wire the oranges and kumquats, push a piece of floral wire through the fruit near one end. Bring the wire ends together and twist them tightly close to the fruit. Don't clip the wires. Gather the kumquats into bunches of five and twist their wires together.

4 Refer to the photo *above left* for guidance and attach the pinecones, oranges, and kumquat clusters. Twist the wires tightly around the vines on the back of the wreath.

5 Glue the orange slices and cinnamon sticks in place. Cut long orange-peel curls from the remaining oranges and drape them as shown.

Magnolia Wreath

here's how...

1 Wire clusters of magnolia leaves to the grapevine wreath, working counterclockwise and pointing all the stem ends in the same direction. Pack the clusters tightly so the wreath looks very full.

2 Secure the clementines, pomegranates, and apples on floral wire by pushing a piece of wire through the fruit from side to side. Twist the wire ends together tightly at the base of the fruit, leaving the wires long to form a tail. Refer to the photo for placement and position the fruits on the wreath, nestling them down into the magnolia leaves. Push the wire tail through to the back of the wreath and twist it around the grapevine. Cut off any excess wire so it's flush with the back of the wreath.

3 Attach the kumquats and nuts to the wreath with hotmelt adhesive.

4 To make a hanging loop, fold a piece of floral wire in half and wrap it tightly around the vines at the back of the wreath.

43

SHOPPING LIST:

From a crafts store:
   medium-weight
     floral wire
   24-inch-diameter
     grapevine wreath (or
     smaller, if desired)
   hot-glue gun and
     glue sticks
From your yard:
   clusters of fresh
     magnolia leaves
From a grocer:
   fresh fruits such as
     kumquats, clementines
     (a tangerinelike fruit),
     pomegranates, apples
   mixed in-shell nuts

Bay Leaves and Limes

here's how...

1 Cut the bay into short sprigs and attach each sprig to a wooden pick with floral wire.

2 Insert the picks into the grapevine wreath, securing them with hotmelt adhesive. Work in one direction until the grapevine is completely covered.

3 Referring to the photo for guidance, glue the plastic grapes and artificial limes to the wreath.

SHOPPING LIST:

From a crafts store:
12-inch brass ring
(as for macramé)
26-gauge wire
on a spool or
paddle
large-eye embroidery
or tapestry needle
From a grocer:
about 20 fresh
kumquats
From a florist:
branches of
medium-size
broadleaf
evergreen leaves
such as photinia or
laurel

3 Cut a length of wire to fit around the brass ring plus 6 inches. Thread the needle with the wire, then pierce a kumquat with the needle, going through the middle of the fruit from side to side (rather than from blossom end to stem end). Thread the kumquats onto the wire until you have enough to cover the ring. Wrap the wire ends together and cut off the excess.

Kumquat Ring

here's how...

1 Cut the branches of leaves into sprigs about 3 to 4 inches long. Lay one sprig along the outside of the brass ring and wire it to the ring, wrapping the wire along the lower inch of the stem. Do not cut the wire.

2 Lay a second sprig over the stem end of the first, covering the wired portion. Wrap the wire down around the stem to secure it to the ring. Continue wiring sprigs in this manner until the brass ring is covered. Hide the stem of the last sprig under the top of the first sprig.

4 Attach the kumquat necklace to the leaf-covered brass ring with additional wire, carefully working it between the kumquats.

45

Holly and Ivy

SHOPPING LIST:

12- to 14-inch diameter
metal ring
10 to 12 ivy vines
sprigs of holly with
red berries
lightweight floral wire

here's how...

1 Wire the fresh ivy vines to the metal ring, arranging them to cover it completely. Let the vines at the bottom hang more loosely for a natural look.

2 To create a focal point, add extra vines around the bottom half of the ring. Allow some of the vines to extend across the opening toward the back of the wreath to give it visual depth.

3 Wire sprigs of holly berries at the bottom to make a "bow."

Perk up sofas and chairs with special pillows. Department stores and gift catalogs offer package-shaped and novelty pillows for the holidays, but it's easy to make your own.

holiday pillows

46

If you're short on time, buy solid-color throw pillows and glue on a ring of silk ivy for a quick holiday face-lift; or make a corsage from silk poinsettias that you can remove after the holidays.

If you have a little more time, make your own pillows and decorate them with snowy lace or with snowflakes cut from fusible interfacing. The fusible-interfacing snowflakes are simply ironed onto the fabric, then covered with organdy for a frosty look. Because the motif isn't specific to Hanukkah or Christmas, you can leave these pillows out after the holidays for a winter-season decorating accent.

Ivy Wreath

here's how...

1 Clip the plastic stems from the ivy leaves. Mix equal parts textile medium and gold acrylic paint and apply the mixture to the leaves.

2 After the paint dries, glue the ivy leaves to the front of the pillow with thick white crafts glue.

3 Tie the ribbon into a bow and glue it to the wreath.

Poinsettia Corsage

here's how...

1 Remove the poinsettia petals and one or two leaves from the stem. Beginning with the largest petals, glue the center vein of each petal to the felt circle. Glue smaller petals over the large petals to re-create the flower. Glue one or two leaves under the petals.

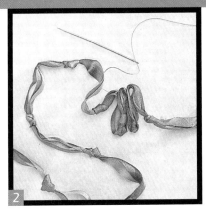

To make the flower center, hold the three ribbons together as one. Beginning 1 inch from one end, knot the ribbons every 1½ inches until you reach the opposite end.

3 Draw a threaded needle through one end of the knotted ribbon strand. Bring the knots together, folding the ribbon as you would a paper fan. Stitch through the V folds between the knots with the needle and thread. Pull the thread tightly and knot it to secure the ribbon pompom.

4 Glue the ribbon pompom to the center of the poinsettia. After the glue dries, use small safety pins to attach the corsage to the pillow.

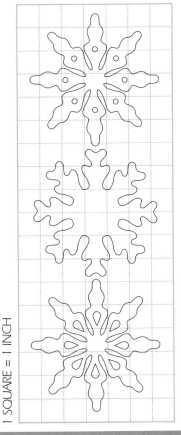

1 SQUARE = 1 INCH

SHOPPING LIST:

⅓ yard of raspberry linen
10x16-inch piece
    of organdy
scraps of white fusible
    interfacing for snowflakes
three 2-inch-diameter
    lace medallions
1½ yards of
    ¼-inch-diameter
    cording for piping
½ yard of linen or
    cotton for the piping
matching thread
purchased or pre-made
    pillow form

Snowflake Pillow

here's how...

1 Enlarge the snowflake patterns *below* to scale (445 percent on a copier). Trace them onto the interfacing, and cut them out.

Cut two 10x16-inch pieces of linen. Fuse the snowflakes to one piece, following the manufacturer's instructions. Tack the lace medallions to the fabric, too.

Baste the organdy rectangle over the pillow front.

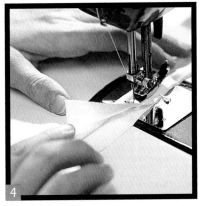

Cut and piece 3-inch-wide bias-cut strips of linen or cotton fabric to measure 1½ yards long. Cover the cording with this strip, then baste the covered cording to the pillow front along the seam line, with raw edges aligned.

5 Sew the pillow front to the pillow back, right sides facing, leaving an opening along one side. Trim the seams, clip the corners, and turn the pillow right side out. Insert the pillow form, and blind-stitch the opening closed.

47

Add cozy warmth with accent lamps. Place one in a powder room or bedroom, tuck one into a bookshelf, or use a matching pair on a mantel. They make great gifts, too.

shed a little *light*

To make these lamps, simply adhere paper onto a purchased shade. Look for self-adhesive lampshades at fabric stores, or buy inexpensive fabric-covered shades from a discount store. To adapt the shades for use with candles, look for candle followers at lamp and lighting stores.

SHOPPING LIST

small lampshade
crafts knife or scissors
old sheet music, pictures,
    or computer-generated
    Christmas carol lyrics
white crafts glue
paintbrush
water-base varnish
fine sandpaper
tack cloth
gold leaf and adhesive size
decorative trims, such as
    cording or tassel fringe

Lyrical Lampshade

here's how...

1 With a crafts knife or scissors, cut out sheet music, pictures, or computer-generated Christmas carol lyrics, using only noncopyrighted images.

2 Lay out the pieces and lightly mark their positions on the lampshade before permanently applying them.

3 Mix a little water with the crafts glue so it will spread easily. Apply the glue-water solution to the back of the sheet music and pictures with a paintbrush. Carefully smooth the pieces onto the lampshade and allow to dry.

4 Apply three coats of the water-base varnish over the lampshade. Let each coat dry, then sand lightly and wipe with the tack cloth before applying the next coat. Apply gold leaf to the top and bottom edges of the shade, using adhesive size and following the manufacturer's instructions. Glue a length of tassel fringe or cording around the bottom inside edge of the shade.

"Joy to the World" Lampshade

SHOPPING LIST

small bowl
needle-nose pliers
wire cutters
From a crafts store:
   paintbrush
   white crafts glue
   19-gauge and
     24-gauge wire
From a fabric store:
   small lampshade (about
     8 inches high and 10
     inches in diameter at
     the base)
From an art supply store:
   fiber paper: one sheet
     each of green, yellow,
     black, red, blue,
     and white

here's how...

1 From the green paper, tear four tree shapes, making them about 2½ inches tall. From yellow paper, tear four 1-inch-wide stars. From black paper, tear four rectangles about ½ inch high for tree trunks. From red paper, tear small circles for ornaments. For the worlds, tear four large blue circles and a variety of green shapes for land masses. Tear white paper into ½-inch pieces to cover the background.

If you use a self-adhesive lampshade, peel away the paper and adhere the four trees around the upper half of the shade, spacing them evenly. Press a star to the top of each tree and a trunk to the bottom of each tree. Press a blue world below each trunk. (If you use a plain fabric-covered shade, glue the shapes to the shade with a solution of equal parts of glue and water.)

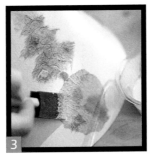

Mix equal parts of glue and water in a small bowl and glue paper ornaments to the trees and the land masses to the worlds.

4 Press the ½-inch pieces of white paper onto the shade wherever the adhesive surface is still exposed. (If you use a fabric shade, this step isn't necessary, but you will need to paint the exposed fabric with the glue solution. Otherwise, when the lamp is turned on, you'll see the glue around the shapes.)

5 Paint the entire surface with the glue-water mixture to adhere any loose edges and to seal and varnish the shade.

For the wire words, first write "Joy to the World" in cursive on a piece of paper. Bend 19-gauge wire with needle-nose pliers, using the written words as a template.

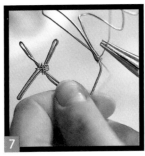

Reinforce joints or intersection points by wrapping them with 24-gauge wire.

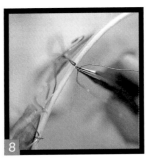

Position the four wire words evenly around the shade. Loop the 24-gauge wire around the two or three tallest parts of each word. Poke small holes at the base of the shade and run the wire through the holes. Twist to secure, and then trim any excess wire with the wire cutters.

9 Bend the 19-gauge wire into four small stars. Attach the stars between the wire words in the same manner as directed in Step 8.

Dip the remaining bits of fiber paper into the glue solution, and wring them dry between your fingers. Wrap these strips randomly around the letters and stars.

49

Santa wouldn't dare put sticks and coal in this stocking or the one on the following page. Stitched from velvet and damask, they're easy to make—and sure proof that you've been good.

stockings
with style

Both stockings require only basic sewing skills, but for an even quicker alternative, start with plain purchased stockings and add ribbon streamers or upholstery fringe.

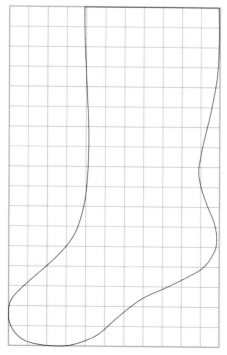

1 SQUARE = 1 INCH

Ribbon-Fringed Stocking

❧ Finished size is approximately 17 inches.

here's how...

1 Enlarge the pattern *at left* by drawing a grid of 1-inch squares and copying the lines, square by square, from the pattern. Or enlarge it 485 percent on a copier—this will require several passes.

2 Fold the velvet in half with right sides facing, and trace the pattern on the wrong side of the fabric.

3 Sew along the drawn line, leaving the top straight edge unstitched. Cut along the top straight edge and then ½ inch beyond the stitched line. Clip the curves and turn the stocking right side out.

4 Cut the organdy ribbons into 8-inch lengths for the fringe. Pin two layers of the organdy ribbons around the top of the stocking, matching one short end of each ribbon to the raw edge of the stocking; baste in place.

5 Cut the gold ribbon into one 8-inch and two 6-inch lengths. (Set the remaining 7 inches of ribbon aside for the hanger.) Thread the 8-inch length through the loop on the large star charm and glue the ribbon end in place to secure the charm. Repeat for the small star charms on the 6-inch lengths. Baste the free ends of the ribbons to the ribbon cuff.

6 Fold the remaining 7 inches of gold ribbon in half for a hanger. Sew the hanger to the top corner of the stocking, matching raw edges.

¾ yard of red velvet
¾ yard of lining fabric
matching thread
dressmaker's chalk
3 yards each of two
    1- or 2-inch-wide
    coordinating white-and-
    gold organdy ribbons
3 yards of 1-inch-wide
    white organdy ribbon
¾ yard of ⅛-inch-wide
    gold satin ribbon
one large and two small
    brass star charms
fabric glue

7 Stitch and cut out the lining as directed for the stocking, leaving an opening at the bottom for turning. Do not turn.

8 Slip the stocking into the lining with the right sides facing. Sew around the upper edge of the cuff.

9 Turn the stocking right side out through the opening in the bottom of the lining. Slip-stitch the opening closed. Tuck the lining inside.

10 Trim the ribbon fringe to varying lengths.

51

52

Damask Stocking

❧ Finished size is approximately 17 inches.

here's how...

1 Enlarge the pattern on *page 50* as directed in step 1 of the Ribbon-Fringed Stocking.

2 Cut the damask fabric into two ½-yard pieces. From one of the pieces, cut and piece 2-inch-wide bias strips to cover enough cording to outline the stocking. Fold the bias strip over the cording and stitch close to the cording.

3 Cut two 13x20-inch rectangles *each* from the remaining piece of damask and the fleece. Pin a fleece rectangle to the wrong side of each damask rectangle, leaving 2 inches of damask exposed at one short end. This will be the top hemmed edge of the stocking. Trim excess fleece at the bottom edge. Fuse the fleece to the damask.

4 Place the fabric rectangles together, right sides facing, and pin the pattern on top, aligning the top edge of the pattern with the fleece edge at the top. Cut out the stocking front and back, adding a ½-inch seam to the sides and bottom. Set the pieces aside.

Fold the top raw edge of each stocking piece under ½ inch. Fold under again 1½ inches.

Stitch close to the fold.

Align one end of the piping with the top edge of the stocking front. Pin, then stitch the piping to the stocking front along the seam line. Trim away any excess piping.

With the right sides facing, sew the stocking front to the stocking back along the seam line. Clip the curves, and turn the stocking right side out.

9 Cut a 3x6-inch hanger strip from the damask fabric. Press under ½ inch on the long edges of the strip, and topstitch in place. Fold the strip in half crosswise and tack to the back of the stocking.

Pin, then sew the fringe around the upper edge of the stocking.

For the roses: To make the center of the rose, wrap the organdy ribbon tightly around a pencil 12 times. Do not cut the ribbon.

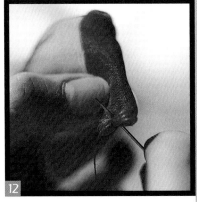

Slide the ribbon off and hand-tack one end closed.

To make the petals, loosely twist the ribbon tail into loops, bringing the ribbon back to the tacked center at the end of each loop. Tack each petal in place. Continue making petals until the roses are the desired shape and size. Tack securely and trim the end.

14 For leaves: Cut the velvet ribbon into 4-inch lengths. Fold each length in half crosswise, right sides facing. Sew from one corner of the top folded edge diagonally to the center on the other side. Trim excess ribbon and turn the leaf right side out.

15 Tack the leaves and roses to the cuff.

53

Make a few of these for your own home, or craft a whole collection so you'll have some to keep and some to share.

ornaments
on display

Christmas ornaments don't just hang on the tree anymore. Tie them into wreaths and garlands, pile them in bowls, or perch them on candlesticks for a festive display. Use the whimsical wire Christmas tree as a package topper, or make several trees to hang from a café curtain rod in front of a window.

54

SHOPPING LIST:
From a crafts store:
 white crafts glue
 paintbrush
 papier-mâché stars
 pepper berries (also
  available at floral-
  supply shops)
 gold cord (optional)
 plastic-foam balls
 masking tape
 ribbon (optional)
From a health-food store
 (or the spice section of a
 grocery store):
 star anise, cinnamon
  pieces, whole cloves,
  and dried orange and
  lemon peel

Spicy Stars

here's how...

1 Thin the crafts glue with water to the consistency of cream. Using the paintbrush, cover the stars with the glue.

2 While the glue is still wet, press the stars into pepper berries or star anise.

3 Glue additional pepper berries or star anise to the star shapes where needed.

4 Trim stars with gold cord, if desired.

Spice-Covered Spheres

here's how...

1 Cover the plastic-foam balls with masking tape.

2 Thin the crafts glue with water to the consistency of cream. Using the paintbrush, cover the taped surface with the glue.

3 While the glue is still wet, roll the ball in star anise, cinnamon pieces, whole cloves, and orange and lemon peel.

4 Trim the spheres with ribbon, if desired.

SHOPPING LIST:
glass Christmas
    balls
paper towel
gift wrap
From a crafts store:
star paper punch
thick crafts glue
Delta Ceramcoat
    Fine Crackle
    Finish
acrylic crafts
    paints: gold,
    silver
paintbrush

Beaded-Wire Tree

here's how...

1 Englarge the pattern *below* 200 to 225 percent on a copier. Transfer the pattern to the scrap of wood using graphite paper and a stylus or ballpoint pen.

2 Hammer nails into the wood, part way, at the points indicated on the pattern.

3 Wrap the 20-gauge wire around the nails four times to outline the tree shape.

4 Carefully remove the nails from the wood and the ornament, then wrap the cut wire ends around the tree form to secure it.

5 Wrap the 24-gauge wire around and across the tree shape, randomly adding glass beads. Crimp the wire to hold the beads in place. Wrap the wire ends around the tree form to secure them.

6 To hang the ornament, thread an 8-inch length of embroidery floss through the top of the ornament and knot the ends together.

SHOPPING LIST:
scrap of wood
    (at least 4x5 inches)
graphite paper and a
    stylus (from an art-supply
    store) or ballpoint pen
hammer and nails
    (7 for each ornament)
silver wire: 20- and 24-gauge
wire clippers
assorted glass beads
embroidery floss for
    a hanger

Nail Placements

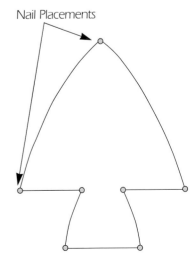

Crackled Christmas Balls

here's how...

1 Wash and dry the Christmas balls.

2 Use the paper punch to punch stars from the gift wrap. Randomly glue the paper stars to the balls.

3 Following the manufacturer's instructions, brush crackle medium over each ball. To let the balls dry, hang them on a folding wooden clothes-drying rack or a clothesline stretched taut; place newspapers underneath to catch any drips. Use ornament hangers to suspend the balls.

4 After the crackle medium dries, dip the paper towel in the gold and silver paints and dab or swirl them over the ball. If desired, wipe off the excess paint, leaving paint only in the cracks. Let the paint dry.

Romance your rooms with the cozy glow of candlelight.
Purchased candles are easy to personalize, or craft your own.

illuminating
ideas

Poinsettia and Holly Candles

here's how...

1 Trace the pattern pieces *below* onto the appropriate colors of tissue paper. Cut as many shapes as needed to decorate the candle.

2 Position holly leaves and berries or poinsettia petals and center "berries" on the candle.

3 Brush decoupage medium over the motifs to secure them to the candle. Also brush medium over the entire candle surface. Let the candle dry.

4 Use the green acrylic paint to paint veins on the holly leaves.

SHOPPING LIST

tissue paper: red, yellow, and green
pillar candles
decoupage medium
paintbrush
green acrylic paint (for holly candle only)

Give purchased pillar candles a handmade touch by gluing on tissue paper in holiday shapes. Choose fragrant candles scented with pine or bayberry so they'll smell as festive as they look.

The milk-carton candles on *page 57* update a 1970s craft with a twist: use a taper candle instead of candle wicking. For fun, add a sprinkling of glitter before pouring the melted wax.

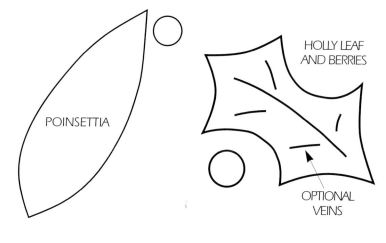

POINSETTIA

HOLLY LEAF
AND BERRIES

OPTIONAL
VEINS

SHOPPING LIST:

clean half-gallon cardboard
    milk carton
a pan and a large
    clean can
broken ice
10-inch white taper candle
large spoon
From a crafts store:
2½ to 3 pounds of wax
    and ¾ cup of stearin
    (to make the wax burn
    better) or use 2½ to 3
    pounds of wax or wax
    crystals with hardener
    already added
candlemaking thermometer
superfine glitter

Milk Carton Candles

here's how...

1 Break the wax into chunks and place it in the can. Pour a few inches of water in the pan, then set the can of wax in the water. Bring the water to simmering and let the wax melt. (To make pouring the wax easier, you may wish to bend the can at the top to form a spout before putting the wax in.)

2 Add stearin to the melted wax. If you're using wax crystals or wax with hardener added, follow the manufacturer's instructions for melting.

Partially fill the milk carton with broken ice cubes. Center a taper in the milk carton, then continue filling the carton with ice. Tap the carton on your work surface to settle the ice, then add more ice. Sprinkle glitter over the ice.

4 Let the wax cool to 170 degrees, then pour it into the carton. As the wax cools and shrinks, add more ice or wax to keep the top of the candle level.

5 After the wax hardens completely, peel the cardboard carton away from the sides. Trim the top of the taper so it's level with the top of the candle, leaving ½ inch of wick. If the bottom of the candle isn't level, slide it across an old warm skillet to smooth any rough spots.

Caution: Wax is extremely flammable. Never melt wax directly over heat or to a temperature above 220 degrees. Never leave melting wax unattended; if it starts to smoke, remove the pan from the heat immediately. If wax catches fire, smother the flame with a pan lid; don't throw water on the flame. Never leave a burning candle unattended, and never burn candles where the flame might come in contact with flammable surfaces or objects.

57

58

Arrange a collar of magnolia leaves on a sconce, holding them in place with a short pillar candle. Add a sprig of pepper berries for color.

Candle lovers take note! Be sure to keep wicks trimmed to prevent the release of soot. If you burn candles often and don't keep the wicks trimmed short, some candles may release enough soot to damage furnishings, fabrics, and ceilings.

In a Twinkling: Candles

▲ An antique muffin tray makes a rustic base for a bed of votives. Tuck holly and berries around each candle, or use two colors of candles and arrange them in a checkerboard pattern. (An old muffin tin will work, too.)

▲ Give purchased pillar candles a handcrafted designer look by adhering pressed or glycerinized leaves to the surface. Spray the candle with spray adhesive and press the leaves in place. Melt candle wax in an old double boiler and paint the entire candle with two coats of wax, letting the wax cool between coats. After the wax has cooled completely, carefully scrape off the top layer with a paring knife so the surface is uneven, allowing the leaves to show more in some areas than in others.

◀ Make instant seasonal candles by filling flea-market teacups and holiday mugs with wax crystals, available at crafts stores. Insert the wick into the center and trim it to ¼ inch above the wax. As the candle burns, the crystals around the wick will melt, but the outer crystals remain loose, so you can pull out the wick "plug," save the remaining wax crystals, and wash out the cup with hot water.

▼ Dress up purchased pillar candles with assorted natural materials. Use floral tape or a rubber band to hold greenery, twigs, or gilded seedpods around the base, then tie raffia or ribbon over the rubber band.

59

▲ Create your own "antique" candles by applying gold or silver metal leaf to purchased pillar candles. Look for metal leaf and spray adhesive size at crafts stores; spritz the candle surface randomly with the size and let it dry a few minutes, until it's tacky. Apply a sheet of metal leaf to the surface and gently rub it to adhere it. Wipe off the metal leaf from unsprayed areas for an aged look.

◀ Bring a warm glow to any dark corner with votive candles dropped into unexpected containers. Any clear glass vessel can work; just be sure there's room around the candle so the flame does not burn close to the glass.

If the holidays inspire you to sing "Food, *glorious food*" from the musical *Oliver*, you'll enjoy the recipes on the following pages. From tasty beginnings to sweet endings, you'll find recipes to mix and match for parties, family meals, and gift-giving. If you're planning a dinner party, use the buffet menu and planning guide to get started. Or welcome the new year with festive dishes and drinks, including good-luck foods and tasty nonalcoholic alternatives to champagne. Let baking be the excuse for a party, and have friends over to decorate cookies. Whatever the menu, let the gathering be joyful!

GATHER

NG *together*

menu

Minestrone
or
Nacho Cheese and
Corn Chowder

❋

Citrus Tossed Salad
with Cranberry
Vinaigrette

❋

Sweet Potato-
Wheat Twist
or
Easy Herb Focaccia

❋

Pumpkin
Gingerbread

❋

Coffee and/or Milk

2

Minestrone

Sweet Potato-Wheat Twist
(see recipe, page 64)

*Citrus Tossed Salad with
Cranberry Vinaigrette*
(see recipe, page 65)

This is a season of stories. Whether it's the Christmas story of Christ's birth or one of the many secular poems and tales that have become Christmas traditions, stories are passed on from one generation to the next.

storyteller's *eve*

Give your family a special gift this year by setting aside an evening for storytelling, complete with a soup supper. Then gather in front of a toasty fire and take turns reading aloud from a favorite book.

Minestrone

Serve this vegetable-packed soup with an assortment of cold cuts, such as salami and ham, a variety of cheeses, olives, and pickled peppers.

- 6 cups water
- 1 28-ounce can tomatoes, cut up
- 1 8-ounce can tomato sauce
- 1 large onion, chopped
- 1 cup chopped cabbage
- 1 medium carrot, chopped
- 1 stalk celery, chopped
- 4 teaspoons instant beef bouillon granules
- 1 tablespoon dried Italian seasoning, crushed
- 1 teaspoon bottled minced garlic or 2 cloves garlic, minced
- ¼ teaspoon pepper
- 1 15-ounce can cannellini or great northern beans
- 1 10-ounce package frozen lima beans or one 9-ounce package frozen Italian-style green beans
- 4 ounces packaged dried linguine or spaghetti, broken
- 1 small zucchini, halved lengthwise and sliced
- 2 to 3 tablespoons purchased pesto (optional)
  Grated Parmesan cheese

Combine water, undrained tomatoes, tomato sauce, onion, cabbage, carrot, celery, bouillon, Italian seasoning, garlic, and pepper in a 5- to 6-quart Dutch oven. Bring to boiling; reduce heat. Cover and simmer 10 minutes.

Stir in undrained canned beans, lima beans, linguine, and zucchini. Return to boiling; reduce heat. Simmer, uncovered, 15 minutes. Serve in bowls. Top each serving with 1 teaspoon pesto, if desired. Pass Parmesan cheese to sprinkle over soup. Makes 8 servings.

Nutrition facts per serving: 177 cal., 3 g total fat (1 g sat. fat), 5 mg chol., 992 mg sodium, 32 g carbo., 5 g fiber, 10 g pro. Daily values: 33% vit. A, 41% vit. C, 14% calcium, 19% iron

Nacho Cheese and Corn Chowder

- 3 medium onions, chopped (1½ cups)
- 6 cups milk
- ¾ cup all-purpose flour
- 4½ teaspoons instant chicken bouillon granules
- 3 cups frozen whole kernel corn
- 3 cups shredded colby-and-Monterey Jack cheese (12 ounces)
- 3 cups shredded American cheese (12 ounces)
- 1 4½-ounce can diced green chili peppers, drained
- ½ cup thick and chunky salsa
  Tortilla chips (optional)
  Bottled hot pepper sauce (optional)

Combine onions and 3 cups water in a 4½- to 5-quart Dutch oven. Bring to boiling; reduce heat. Cover and simmer about 5 minutes or until onions are tender. *Do not drain.*

Gradually stir or whisk 2 cups of the milk into the flour until smooth. Stir into Dutch oven with remaining milk and bouillon granules. Cook and stir over medium heat until thickened and bubbly. Cook and stir 1 minute more.

Stir in corn, cheeses, and chili peppers. Cook over low heat, stirring frequently, until heated through. Garnish each serving with 1 tablespoon salsa and a few tortilla chips, if desired. Pass hot pepper sauce, if desired. Makes 8 servings.

Nutrition facts per serving: 485 cal., 27 g total fat (16 g sat. fat), 77 mg chol., 1,490 mg sodium, 37 g carbo., 1 g fiber, 27 g pro. Daily values: 36% vit. A, 24% vit. C, 66% calcium, 11% iron

Easy Herb Focaccia

This simplified version of focaccia (foh CAH chee ah) starts with a roll mix.

1 16-ounce package hot roll mix
1 egg
2 tablespoons olive oil
⅔ cup finely chopped onion
1 teaspoon dried rosemary, crushed
2 teaspoons olive oil

Lightly grease one 15×10×1-inch baking pan, one 12- to 14-inch pizza pan, or two 9×1½-inch round baking pans. Set aside.

Prepare the hot roll mix according to package directions for basic dough, using the 1 egg and substituting the 2 tablespoons oil for the margarine. Knead dough; allow to rest as directed. If using large baking pan, roll dough into a 15×10-inch rectangle and carefully transfer to prepared pan. If using a pizza pan, roll dough into a 12-inch round. For round baking pans, divide dough in half; roll into two 9-inch rounds. Place in prepared pan(s).

Cook onion and rosemary in the 2 teaspoons oil in a skillet until onion is tender. With fingertips, press indentations every inch or so in dough. Top dough evenly with onion mixture. Cover; let rise in a warm place until nearly double (about 30 minutes).

Bake in a 375° oven for 15 to 20 minutes or until golden. Cool 10 minutes on a wire rack(s). Remove from pan(s) and cool completely. Makes 24 servings.

Nutrition facts per serving: 85 cal., 2 g total fat (0 g sat. fat), 9 mg chol., 133 mg sodium, 14 g carbo., 0 g fiber, 2 g pro. Daily values: 1% vit. A, 0% vit. C, 0% calcium, 4% iron

Sweet Potato-Wheat Twist

Wrap one loaf in heavy foil or place in a freezer bag and freeze up to 3 months (see photo, page 62).

1¼ cups water
1 cup chopped peeled sweet potato (1 medium)
1 cup buttermilk
2 tablespoons shortening, margarine, or butter
2 tablespoons honey
2 teaspoons salt
4¾ to 5½ cups all-purpose flour
2 packages active dry yeast
1 egg
1½ cups whole wheat flour

Combine water and sweet potato in a medium saucepan. Bring to boiling; reduce heat. Cover and simmer about 12 minutes or until very tender. *Do not drain.* Mash potato in the water. Measure potato-water mixture and, if necessary, add water to equal 1½ cups.

Return potato mixture to saucepan. Add buttermilk, shortening, honey, and salt. Heat or cool, as necessary, and stir until warm (120° to 130°).

Stir together 2 cups of the all-purpose flour and the yeast in a large mixing bowl. Add potato mixture and egg. Beat with an electric mixer on low speed for 30 seconds, scraping the sides of the bowl constantly. Beat on high speed for 3 minutes. Divide the batter in half.

To half of the batter, stir in the whole wheat flour and about ½ cup all-purpose flour, using a spoon. Turn out onto a lightly floured surface. Knead in enough flour (¼ to ½ cup) to make a moderately stiff dough that is smooth and elastic (6 to 8 minutes total). Shape into a ball. Place in a lightly greased bowl; turn once to grease surface. Cover and let rise in a warm place until double (about 45 minutes).

To the remaining batter, stir in as much of the remaining all-purpose flour as you can (about 2 cups), using a spoon. Turn out onto a lightly floured surface. Knead in enough of the remaining flour (¼ to ½ cup) to make a moderately stiff dough that is smooth and elastic (6 to 8 minutes total). Shape into a ball. Place in a lightly greased bowl; turn once to grease surface. Cover and let rise in a warm place until double (about 45 minutes).

Punch each ball of dough down and turn out onto a lightly floured surface. Divide each ball of dough in half. Cover and let rest for 10 minutes.

Roll each portion of dough into an evenly thick 10-inch-long rope. Loosely twist one plain and one whole wheat rope together; press ends together to seal. Place in a lightly greased 9×5×3-inch loaf pan. Repeat with remaining two ropes in another loaf pan. Cover and let rise in a warm place until nearly double (30 to 40 minutes).

Bake in a 375° oven about 40 minutes or until breads sound hollow when lightly tapped. If necessary, loosely cover bread with foil the last 10 minutes to prevent overbrowning. Remove from pans immediately. Cool on wire racks. Makes 2 loaves (32 slices).

Nutrition facts per slice: 103 cal., 1 g total fat (0 g sat. fat), 7 mg chol., 145 mg sodium, 20 g carbo., 1 g fiber, 3 g pro. Daily values: 8% vit. A, 1% vit. C, 1% calcium, 7% iron

64

Pumpkin Gingerbread

Citrus Tossed Salad *with* Cranberry Vinaigrette

See photo, page 62.

8 cups torn mixed greens
2 cups orange sections and/or
     red grapefruit sections
2 cups jicama, cut into thin,
     bite-size strips
2 small red onions, sliced and
     separated into rings
     Cranberry Vinaigrette
     Croutons (optional)

Combine torn mixed greens, orange and/or grapefruit sections, jicama, and red onions in a large salad bowl. Shake Cranberry Vinaigrette well. Pour over salad. Toss lightly to coat. If desired, top with croutons. Serve immediately. Makes 8 servings.

CRANBERRY VINAIGRETTE: Combine ½ cup cranberry juice; 2 tablespoons salad oil; 2 tablespoons vinegar; 2 teaspoons snipped fresh basil or ½ teaspoon dried basil, crushed; and 1 teaspoon sugar in screw-top jar. Cover and shake well. Makes about ⅔ cup.

Nutrition facts per serving: 94 cal., 4 g total fat (1 g sat. fat), 0 mg chol., 6 mg sodium, 15 g carbo., 2 g fiber, 2 g pro. Daily values: 11% vit. A, 76% vit. C, 4% calcium, 7% iron

Pumpkin Gingerbread

1¼ cups all-purpose flour
1½ teaspoons grated fresh
      gingerroot or ½ teaspoon
      ground ginger
1 teaspoon finely shredded
     orange peel
¾ teaspoon ground cinnamon

½ teaspoon baking powder
½ teaspoon baking soda
⅓ cup butter
⅓ cup packed brown sugar
1 egg
½ cup canned pumpkin
¼ cup mild-flavored molasses
¼ cup milk
     Whipped cream
     Orange peel curls (optional)

Stir together flour, gingerroot or ground ginger, finely shredded orange peel, cinnamon, baking powder, and baking soda in a medium mixing bowl. Set aside.

Beat together butter and brown sugar in a large mixing bowl with an electric mixer on medium to high speed until combined. Add egg and beat well. Beat in pumpkin and molasses on medium speed until smooth.

Alternately add flour mixture and milk to the pumpkin mixture, beating until smooth. Pour into a greased and lightly floured 8×8×2-inch baking pan.

Bake in a 350° oven for 35 to 40 minutes or until a wooden toothpick inserted near center comes out clean. Cool in pan on a wire rack 10 minutes. Serve warm with whipped cream. If desired, garnish with orange peel curls. Makes 9 servings.

Nutrition facts per serving: 233 cal., 13 g total fat (8 g sat. fat), 63 mg chol., 179 mg sodium, 27 g carbo., 1 g fiber, 3 g pro. Daily values: 44% vit. A, 1% vit. C, 5% calcium, 11% iron

65

Try These for a Good Read

If you don't have a favorite for family reading, try one of the following titles recommended by children's literature consultant Susannah Richards.

collections

A CHRISTMAS TREASURY selected by Stephanie Nettell, illustrated by Ian Penney (Penguin, 1997, all ages).
An appealing anthology of varied offerings, this collection can be read, enjoyed, and shared by adults and a wide age range of children. It includes poetry, songs, stories, and excerpts of longer works from both traditional and contemporary sources. The book is divided into sections emphasizing the religious aspects of Christ's birth, feasting, the joy of giving and receiving gifts, and reflections and experiences of the holiday from a variety of regions, times, and cultures.

MICHAEL HAGUE'S FAMILY CHRISTMAS TREASURY illustrated by Michael Hague (Henry Holt, 1995, all ages).
Hague, known for his illustrations of works such as *The Secret Garden*, has chosen 32 of his favorite stories, poems, and songs to present with his own illustrations. This well-stocked sampler includes excerpts from *A Christmas Carol*, Kenneth Grahame's *Wind in the Willows*, and *A Child's Christmas in Wales*, as well as O. Henry's "The Gift of the Magi."

CHILDREN JUST LIKE ME: CELEBRATIONS! by Barnabas and Anabel Kindersley (Dorling-Kindersley, 1997, all ages).
Children around the world celebrate 25 favorite holidays in this stunning photographic collection. The details and rituals of each holiday are shared by individual children who bring vibrancy and exuberance to the holiday descriptions.

THE FAMILY TREASURY OF JEWISH HOLIDAYS by Malka Drucker, illustrated by Nancy Patz (Little Brown, 1994, all ages).
This real treasure is not only for the children in the family but for the parents as well. A 10-chapter anthology of Jewish holidays, it is a rich resource that goes well beyond describing ritual to offer a wealth of Jewish history and symbolism. Additionally, it includes related songs, recipes, crafts, and read-along selections by Isaac Bashevis Singer and others.

christmas

SANTA'S BOOK OF NAMES by David McPhail (Little Brown, 1997 [1993], ages 4 to 8).
After Santa accidentally drops his very important list, Edward catches up with him and helps him decipher it. It's a wonderful story with equally delightful ink and watercolor illustrations.

SANTA CALLS by William Joyce (HarperCollins, 1993, ages 5 to 9).
The reader is a guest on an exciting journey to the North Pole. The final twists in this fantastic tale are revealed in two facsimile letters attached at the end of the book.

THE STORY OF CHRISTMAS by Barbara Cooney, illustrated by Loretta Krupinski (Dial, 1995 [1967], ages 3 to 6).
There are many different ways to celebrate Christmas, and Cooney explains the origins of the holiday and of the feasts and celebrations held at that time of year by different faiths and cultures. Many of these customs have been incorporated into Western Christmas traditions. The richness of the holiday is beautifully illustrated in gouache and colored pencil.

THE FIRST CHRISTMAS by Nonny Hogrogian (Greenwillow, 1995, ages 4 and up).
Using passages from the King James Version of the Bible, simple narration to connect them, and lavish oil paintings as illustrations, the author relates the story of the first Christmas. This beautiful retelling of a familiar tale is for readers young and old.

A CHRISTMAS CAROL by Charles Dickens, illustrated by Everett Shinn. (Stewart, Tabori & Chang, 1997, ages 9 and up).
Dickens' Christmas story has been in print for more than 150 years. In this version, his original text is accompanied by Everett Shinn's illustrations for the 1938 edition of *A Christmas Carol* and the 1941 *Christmas in Dickens*. The book's classic design and its time-honored story make this a wonderful family gift as well as a good choice for reading aloud.

THE TWELVE DAYS OF CHRISTMAS illustrated by Jan Brett (PaperStar/Putnam, 1997 [1986], all ages).
Vibrant illustrations and the delightful story-within-a-story make this two treasures in one. The center panels relate to the song while the side panels tell the story of a young couple and their family finding and decorating their holiday tree. An editor's note provides some background about the song, the text, and the music.

66

THE NIGHT BEFORE CHRISTMAS by
Clement C. Moore, illustrated by Ted
Rand (North-South, 1995, all ages).
The classic poem is presented in a
large-format book with beautiful
watercolor illustrations. A perfect
version to share as an annual tradition.

hanukkah

HANUKKAH! by Roni Schotter,
illustrated by Marylin Hafner (Little,
Brown, 1990, ages 4 to 8).
This charming family story has everyone
joining in to prepare the traditional
Hanukkah foods and to participate in
holiday activities. The book concludes
with a brief overview of the holiday and
definitions of some Hanukkah words.

**A GREAT MIRACLE HAPPENED THERE:
A CHANUKAH STORY** by Karla Kuskin,
illustrated by Robert Andrew Parker
(HarperTrophy, 1995 [1993], ages 5
to 8).
A young Jewish boy shares the
celebration of Chanukah with his non-
Jewish friend and explains the meaning
of the holiday to him. The Chanukah
story is one of faith, courage in the face
of insurmountable odds, and victory.

**THE ADVENTURES OF HERSHEL OF
OSTROPOL** by Eric A. Kimmel,
illustrated by Trina Schart Hyman
(Holiday House, 1995, ages 5 and up).
Hershel's adventures are retold by the
master storyteller Kimmel. Hershel
actually lived in the last century, and
stories about him have become folk
tales of a Jewish trickster. He's never
evil and is often laughed at as a fool;
but Hershel is no fool, and stories about
him have lasted for generations.

**WHILE THE CANDLES BURN: EIGHT
STORIES FOR HANUKKAH** by Barbara
Diamond Goldin, illustrated by Elaine
Greenstein (Viking, 1996, ages 4 to 8).

This collection of Jewish stories weaves
the traditional Hanukkah motifs of
miracles and victory in with universal
themes of peace, charity, and religious
commitment. It is an elegant anthology
that spans history, geography, and
cultural tradition.

THE UGLY MENORAH by Marissa Moss
(Farrar, Straus & Giroux, 1996, ages 4
to 8).
Rachel is spending Hanukkah with her
grandmother to keep her company now
that she is a widow. When Rachel sees
her grandmother's very simple "ugly"
menorah, she asks why her
grandmother doesn't get a new one.
What follows is a touching story that
emphasizes warm family memories and
the idea that beauty is indeed in the eye
of the beholder.

kwanzaa

SEVEN CANDLES FOR KWANZAA by
Andrea Davis Pinkney, illustrated by
Brian Pinkney (Dial, 1993, ages 4 to 8).
This book presents a simple explanation
of the principles of Kwanzaa, to be read
while lighting the candles during the
weeklong holiday.

KWANZAA: A FAMILY AFFAIR by
Mildred Pitts Walter, illustrated by
Cheryl Carrington (Lothrop, 1995, ages
7 and up).
This celebrated author provides
background information and shares her
own experiences of Kwanzaa. She also
offers instructions for crafts and recipes
for special holiday dishes.

**THE CHILDREN'S BOOK OF KWANZAA: A
GUIDE TO CELEBRATING THE HOLIDAY**
by Dolores Johnson (Aladdin, 1997,
ages 7 and up).
Johnson's comprehensive book provides
a brief history of Africans and Africans
in America. Chapters detail the seven

principles of Kwanzaa and how they are
practiced, as well as cover the holiday's
symbols and how they are used. Crafts,
gift ideas, and recipes are also included.

A KWANZAA CELEBRATION by Nancy
Williams, illustrated by Robert Sabuda
(Little Simon, 1995, ages 2 and up).
Each spread in this pop-up book
illustrates and describes one of the
principles of Kwanzaa. The text teaches
the symbols and words associated with
the holiday.

CELEBRATING KWANZAA by Diane Hoyt-
Goldsmith, photos by Lawrence
Migdale (Holiday House, 1993, ages 8
to 12).
A Chicago African-American family
celebrates Kwanzaa. The text explains
the origin of the holiday, customs, and
the seven principles. Color photographs
complement the story.

WOOD-HOOPOE WILLIE by Virginia
Kroll, illustrated by Katherine
Roundtree (Charlesbridge, 1995, ages 4
to 8).
A young boy and his grandfather
explore their African-American heritage.
This upbeat, affirming intergenerational
story ends with a Kwanzaa celebration.

67

Holiday Fruit Salad
(see recipe, page 73)

Company Scalloped Potato
(see recipe, page 71)

Green Beans with
Caramelized Onions
(see recipe, page 72)

Festive Pork Roast
(see recipe, page 70)

buffet dinner

Buffets are a great way to entertain larger numbers of people when dining table space is limited. And buffet service allows you to relax with your guests.

Dilly Buns
(see recipe, page 73)

Shrimp with Mustard Cream Sauce

Fresh pea pods dress shrimp in style and make them easier to handle as a finger food (see photo, page 70).

1½ pounds medium shrimp (about 36), peeled and deveined*
36 fresh pea pods
2 tablespoons butter or margarine
4 teaspoons all-purpose flour
½ cup half-and-half or light cream
½ cup dairy sour cream
¼ cup white wine vinegar
2 tablespoons Dijon-style mustard
½ teaspoon pepper
1 tablespoon capers, drained (optional)
Romaine leaves (optional)

Cook shrimp, uncovered, in boiling water about 2 minutes or until opaque. Drain. Cook the pea pods, covered, in a small amount of lightly salted, boiling water for 2 to 3 minutes or until tender. Drain, rinse, and cool. Wrap a pea pod around each shrimp. Secure with a toothpick. Cover and chill.
For sauce, melt butter in a small saucepan. Stir in flour. Add cream all at once. Cook and stir over medium heat until thickened and bubbly. Reduce heat; cook and stir 1 minute more. Remove from heat.
Stir sour cream, vinegar, mustard, and pepper into cream mixture. Pour into a small serving bowl; cover and chill. To serve, sprinkle sauce with capers and serve with shrimp arranged on a platter lined with romaine leaves, if desired. Makes 36 (12 servings).
***Note:** Leave shell on the tails of the shrimp, if desired.

Nutrition facts per serving: 93 cal., 6 g total fat (3 g sat. fat), 77 mg chol., 168 mg sodium, 3 g carbo., 0 g fiber, 8 g pro. Daily values: 8% vit. A, 11% vit. C, 3% calcium, 8% iron

6

menu

Shrimp with Mustard Cream Sauce

✳

Festive Pork Roast

✳

Company Scalloped Potatoes

✳

Green Beans with Caramelized Onions

✳

Holiday Fruit Salad

✳

Dilly Buns – Butter

✳

Mocha-Ladyfinger Parfaits and/or Fruited Nut and Cream Cheese Tart

✳

Choice of beverages

for *twelve*

Shrimp with Mustard Cream Sauce
(see recipe, page 69)

2 teaspoons curry powder
1 teaspoon ground ginger
½ teaspoon pepper
2 tablespoons cornstarch
  Kumquats (optional)
  Fresh herb sprigs (optional)

Place roast in a large plastic bag; set in a large deep bowl. For marinade, combine wine, brown sugar, vinegar, catsup, water, oil, soy sauce, garlic, curry powder, ginger, and pepper in a medium bowl. Pour marinade over meat; seal bag. Marinate in the refrigerator for 6 to 8 hours or overnight, turning the bag several times. Drain meat, reserving marinade in the refrigerator. Pat meat dry.

Place meat on a rack in a shallow roasting pan. Insert meat thermometer. Roast in a 325° oven for 2¼ to 2½ hours or until meat thermometer registers 155°.

About 25 minutes before the meat is done, make sauce. Stir cornstarch into reserved marinade in a medium saucepan. Cook and stir until thickened and bubbly. Cook and stir for 2 minutes more. Brush roast frequently with sauce during the last 15 minutes of roasting.

Let meat stand, covered, about 15 minutes before slicing. (Meat temperature should rise about 5° while standing.) Reheat remaining sauce to boiling and pass with meat. Garnish with kumquats and fresh herbs, such as rosemary, sage, marjoram, and thyme, if desired. Makes 12 to 15 servings.

Nutrition facts per serving: 344 cal., 17 g total fat (5 g sat. fat), 85 mg chol., 394 mg sodium, 16 g carbo., 0 g fiber, 27 g pro. Daily values: 1% vit. A, 4% vit. C, 1% calcium, 11% iron

70

■ Enlisting help: Since buffets tend to be more casual than seated dinners, there's nothing wrong with allowing willing guests to help at any stage of the party. If you wish, assign mini tasks as people arrive. Everyone, including children, can be made to feel more a part of the gathering by being asked to help.

■ Savvy set-up: The more work you do before the party, the more smoothly the plans will flow. Arrange the table in a logical serving sequence starting with plates, followed by the main dish, vegetables, salad, bread, cutlery, and napkins. (To save space, tie cutlery and napkins together with a fancy ribbon.) Appetizers, beverages, and desserts are best set up on separate tables in various locations.

Festive Pork Roast

Ginger, curry, and soy sauce give this pork roast an Oriental accent, and kumquats, used as a garnish, underscore the effect (see photo, pages 68–69).

1 5-pound boneless pork top
  loin roast (double loin, tied)
1½ cups dry red wine
⅔ cup packed brown sugar
½ cup vinegar
½ cup catsup
½ cup water
¼ cup cooking oil
2 tablespoons soy sauce
2 cloves garlic, minced

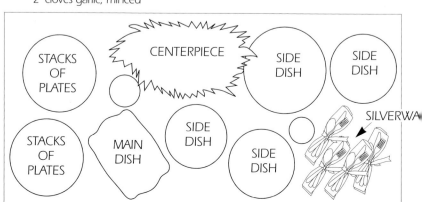

Company Scalloped Potatoes

See photo, pages 68–69.

1 cup chopped onion
¾ cup chopped red and/or green
    sweet pepper (1 medium)
4 cloves garlic, minced
2 tablespoons butter
    or margarine
2 10¾-ounce cans condensed
    cream of celery soup
2 cups milk
¼ teaspoon black pepper
8 cups sliced, peeled potatoes
    (about 2¾ pounds)
⅔ cup grated Parmesan cheese
1 cup soft bread crumbs
3 tablespoons butter
    or margarine, melted
    Green and/or red sweet
    pepper rings (optional)

Cook onion, chopped sweet pepper, and garlic in 2 tablespoons butter or margarine in a large saucepan about 5 minutes or until tender. Stir in soup, milk, and black pepper. Heat, stirring occasionally, until bubbly.

Layer half of the potatoes in a greased 3-quart oval or rectangular baking dish. Cover with *half* of the soup mixture. Sprinkle with *half* of the Parmesan cheese. Layer remaining potatoes and soup mixture atop. Cover dish with foil.

Bake in a 325° oven for 1½ hours or until nearly tender. Uncover and sprinkle with a mixture of bread crumbs, the remaining Parmesan cheese, and melted butter. Bake for 15 minutes more or until potatoes are tender and crumbs are golden. Let stand 15 minutes before serving. Garnish top with sweet pepper rings, if desired. Makes 12 servings.

Nutrition facts per serving: 232 cal., 10 g total fat (5 g sat. fat), 26 mg chol., 590 mg sodium, 30 g carbo., 2 g fiber, 7 g pro. Daily values: 11% vit. A, 22% vit. C, 13% calcium, 5% iron

several days ahead:

■ Have plenty of ice on hand for the chilled beverages. Chill sparkling water, other beverages, and wine, if desired.
■ Make sure that the linens are ironed.
■ Prepare and freeze Dilly Buns.
■ Determine which serving containers will be used.

1 day ahead:

■ Prepare marinade; marinate meat.
■ Prepare mint dressing for Holiday Fruit Salad; cover and chill.
■ For Company Scalloped Potatoes, slice the potatoes and place in cold water in the refrigerator. Chop the onion and sweet pepper and refrigerate in sealed plastic bags. Prepare the crumb mixture and refrigerate in a plastic bag.
■ Prepare the Mocha-Ladyfinger Parfaits and/or the Fruited Nut and Cream Cheese Tart. Cover and chill.
■ Set out the plates, flatware, serving pieces, and glassware. Wrap flatware in napkins and tie with ribbon, if desired.
■ Arrange the centerpiece and gather candles and other table decorations.

up to 8 hours ahead:

■ Cook shrimp and pea pods for Shrimp with Mustard Cream Sauce; wrap shrimp with pea pods. Cover the wrapped shrimp and chill.
■ Prepare sauce for shrimp appetizer; cover and chill in serving bowl.
■ Wash and cut beans and cut onions for Green Beans with Caramelized Onions; refrigerate separately in plastic bags. Toast nuts.
■ Cut butter sticks into pats and place in serving bowl. Cover and chill.

4 hours ahead:

■ Section grapefruit and cut up jicama for Holiday Fruit Salad; cover and chill.

2¾ hours ahead:

■ Set out Dilly Buns to thaw.
■ Start roasting Festive Pork Roast.
■ Prepare Company Scalloped Potatoes, draining off the water in which potatoes were stored. Two hours before serving, add casserole to oven.
■ Arrange shrimp on serving platter; cover and chill until serving time.

1 hour ahead:

■ Cut up avocados and pears for Holiday Fruit Salad and brush with a little orange juice to keep pieces from turning dark. Arrange on romaine-lined platter(s) along with grapefruit and grapes, if desired. Cover and chill.

45 minutes ahead:

■ Prepare sauce for Festive Pork Roast.

30 minutes ahead:

■ Finish preparing Green Beans with Caramelized Onions.

just before serving:

■ Place Dilly Buns in napkin-lined basket or bowl.
■ Add kumquat and fresh herb garnish to the Festive Pork Roast.
■ Sprinkle toasted nuts and bacon over the beans.
■ Add pepper ring garnish to the Company Scalloped Potatoes.
■ Pour salad dressing over salad.
■ Prepare the coffee and/or tea and add any garnishes to the desserts.

71

Green Beans with Caramelized Onions

3 slices bacon

1 tablespoon butter or margarine

4 medium sweet onions, cut into thin wedges

2 cloves garlic, cut into thin slivers

2 teaspoons snipped fresh thyme or ½ teaspoon dried thyme, crushed

2 tablespoons cider vinegar

2 tablespoons brown sugar

2 pounds fresh green beans, washed, trimmed, and cut into 2-inch pieces

¼ cup chopped pecans or almonds, toasted

Cook bacon until crisp in a large skillet. Remove bacon, drain, and crumble, reserving 1 tablespoon of the drippings in the skillet.

Add butter to drippings in skillet. Cook and stir over medium heat until melted. Add onions, garlic, and thyme to skillet. Cover and cook over medium-low heat about 12 minutes or until onions are tender, stirring occasionally. Uncover; add vinegar and sugar. Cook and stir over medium-high heat about 4 minutes or until onions are golden.

Meanwhile, cook green beans in a large saucepan in a small amount of lightly salted water about 10 minutes or just until crisp-tender. Drain.

To serve, toss green beans and onion mixture together. Transfer mixture to a serving bowl. Sprinkle with nuts and crumbled bacon. Makes 12 servings.

Nutrition facts per serving: 73 cal., 3 g total fat (1 g sat. fat), 4 mg chol., 38 mg sodium, 10 g carbo., 2 g fiber, 2 g pro. Daily values: 5% vit. A, 14% vit. C, 3% calcium, 7% iron

Green Beans with Caramelized Onions

72

Dilly Buns

Decorate the tops of these rolls with fresh dill sprigs baked onto the rolls.

- 2½ to 3 cups all-purpose flour
- 1 package fast-rising active dry yeast
- 2 teaspoons dillseed
- ¼ teaspoon baking soda
- 1 cup cream-style cottage cheese
- ¼ cup water
- 2 tablespoons butter or margarine
- 2 teaspoons sugar
- ½ teaspoon salt
- ¼ teaspoon pepper
- 1 egg
- 1 beaten egg
- 1 tablespoon water
  Fresh dill sprigs (optional)

Combine ¾ cup of the flour, the yeast, dillseed, and baking soda in a large mixing bowl. Heat and stir cottage cheese, the ¼ cup water, butter or margarine, sugar, salt, and pepper in a small saucepan until warm (120° to 130°) and butter is almost melted.

Add cheese mixture to flour mixture. Add the first egg. Beat with an electric mixer on low speed for 30 seconds, scraping the sides of the bowl constantly. Beat on high speed for 3 minutes. Using a spoon, stir in as much of the remaining flour as you can.

Turn dough out onto a lightly floured surface. Knead in enough of the remaining flour to make a moderately soft dough that is smooth and elastic (3 to 5 minutes total). Cover and let rest for 15 minutes.

Lightly grease eighteen 2½-inch muffin cups. Shape the dough into 54 balls. (To make 54 equal-size balls, divide entire batch of dough into thirds; divide each portion in half making 6 portions. Divide each of the 6 portions into thirds for 18 portions, and divide each of those 18 portions into thirds, making 54 portions.) Place 3 balls in each muffin cup. Cover; let rise in a warm place until nearly double (20 to 30 minutes).

Combine the remaining beaten egg and 1 tablespoon water; brush onto rolls. Top each roll with a dill sprig, if desired; brush again with egg mixture. Bake in a 375° oven about 12 minutes or until golden. Makes 18 rolls.

Nutrition facts per roll: 93 cal., 2 g total fat (2 g sat. fat), 28 mg chol., 150 mg sodium, 14 g carbo., 1 g fiber, 4 g pro. Daily values: 2% vit. A, 0% vit. C, 1% calcium, 6% iron

Holiday Fruit Salad

If you cut up the pears and avocado ahead, be sure to brush with citrus juice to prevent them from browning (see photo, pages 68–69).

- ¼ cup lime juice
- 2 tablespoons water
- 2 tablespoons salad oil
- 2 teaspoons sugar
- ½ teaspoon celery seed
- 2 teaspoons snipped fresh mint
- 2 medium avocados
  Romaine and/or salad greens
- 1 cup jicama cut into matchstick-size pieces
- 4 large pink grapefruit, peeled and sectioned
- 4 large pears, pared, cored, and sliced (4 cups)
  Red or green grapes (optional)

For dressing, combine lime juice, water, oil, sugar, celery seed, and mint in a screw-top jar. Cover and shake to mix well. Set aside.

Cut avocados lengthwise through the fruit around the seed. Separate halves and remove seed. Peel and slice avocado. Line a large platter (about 16 inches in diameter) with romaine and/or salad greens. Place jicama strips in center of platter. Arrange grapefruit, pear, avocado, and grapes, if desired, around jicama. Shake dressing well; drizzle over salad. Makes 12 servings.

Nutrition facts per serving: 146 cal., 7 g total fat (1 g sat. fat), 0 mg chol., 4 mg sodium, 22 g carbo., 4 g fiber, 2 g pro. Daily values: 7% vit. A, 71% vit. C, 2% calcium, 5% iron

73

Dilly Buns

Fruited Nut and
Cream Cheese Tart

Mocha-Ladyfinger Parfaits

Mocha-Ladyfinger Parfaits

To provide guests with a choice, prepare both the tart and these parfaits.

- 2 4-serving-size packages instant French vanilla pudding mix
- 8 ounces mascarpone cheese or cream cheese
- 1 cup whipping cream
- ⅔ cup strong coffee, cooled
- 1 tablespoon coffee liqueur or hazelnut-flavored syrup (syrup used to flavor coffee)
- 4 ounces milk chocolate or semisweet chocolate
- 2 3-ounce packages ladyfingers (24 ladyfingers), cut crosswise into thirds
- 12 fresh strawberries (optional)

Prepare pudding mixes according to package directions (*using 4 cups milk*). Cover and chill for 2 hours. Meanwhile, let cheese stand at room temperature for 30 minutes.

Stir cheese until smooth. Gradually stir *1 cup* of the pudding into cheese to lighten it. Fold that mixture into the remaining pudding. Beat whipping cream in a chilled small bowl with an electric mixer on medium speed or with a rotary beater just until soft peaks form. Fold whipped cream into pudding mixture; set aside.

Stir together coffee and the coffee liqueur or hazelnut-flavored syrup in a small bowl; set mixture aside. Shave enough curls from the chocolate to sprinkle over tops of the parfaits; finely chop the remaining chocolate.

To assemble parfaits, arrange *half* of the ladyfinger pieces in the bottoms of 12 goblets or glasses. Drizzle *half* of the coffee mixture over ladyfingers in

goblets. Spoon *half* of the pudding mixture on top and sprinkle with chopped chocolate. Repeat with remaining ladyfinger pieces, coffee mixture, and pudding. Top with shaved chocolate curls. Cover and chill about 8 hours or overnight. Garnish each serving with a fresh strawberry, if desired. Makes 12 servings.

Nutrition facts per serving: 353 cal., 22 g total fat (13 g sat. fat), 109 mg chol., 310 mg sodium, 36 g carbo., 1 g fiber, 9 g pro. Daily values: 16% vit. A, 2% vit. C, 10% calcium, 5% iron

Fruited Nut and Cream Cheese Tart

The subtle flavors of dried apricots and nuts come together beautifully in this handsome tart.

    Orange Tart Pastry
- 6 ounces cream cheese, softened
- 1 egg
- 3 tablespoons granulated sugar
- ¼ teaspoon vanilla
- 2 eggs
- ⅔ cup light-colored corn syrup
- ⅓ cup packed brown sugar
- ¼ cup butter or margarine, melted and cooled
- 1 teaspoon finely shredded orange peel
- ½ teaspoon vanilla
- 1 cup coarsely chopped pistachio nuts and/or cashews
- ½ cup snipped dried apricots
    Whipped cream (optional)
    Pistachio nut halves (optional)

Prepare pastry. Use your hands to slightly flatten pastry dough on a lightly floured surface. Roll dough from center to edge into a 13-inch circle. Wrap pastry around rolling pin. Unroll into an ungreased 11-inch tart pan with a removable bottom. Ease pastry into tart pan, being careful not to stretch pastry. Press pastry into the fluted side of tart pan. Trim edge. Place a double

thickness of foil over pastry in the bottom of tart pan. Bake in a 450° oven for 5 minutes; remove foil. Bake 5 minutes more; set aside.

Beat cream cheese, 1 egg, granulated sugar, and ¼ teaspoon vanilla in a small mixing bowl with an electric mixer on medium speed until combined. Cover and chill in refrigerator for 30 minutes. Spread in pastry-lined tart pan.

For filling, beat the 2 eggs slightly in a large mixing bowl with a rotary beater or a fork. Stir in the corn syrup. Add the brown sugar, butter, orange peel, and ½ teaspoon vanilla, stirring until sugar is dissolved. Stir in nuts and apricots.

Place pastry-and-cream-cheese-lined tart pan on a baking sheet on the oven rack. Carefully pour filling into pan. Bake in a 350° oven about 40 minutes or until a knife inserted near the center comes out clean. Cool for 1 to 2 hours on a wire rack. Refrigerate within 2 hours; cover for longer storage. Garnish with whipped cream and pistachio nuts, if desired. Cut into wedges to serve. Makes 12 servings.

ORANGE TART PASTRY: Stir together 1¼ cups all-purpose flour and ¼ cup granulated sugar in a medium mixing bowl. Using a pastry blender, cut in ½ cup cold butter until the pieces are pea-size. Stir together 2 beaten egg yolks, 1 tablespoon water, and 1½ teaspoons finely shredded orange peel in a small mixing bowl. Gradually stir egg yolk mixture into dry mixture. Using your fingers, gently knead dough just until a ball forms. If necessary, cover with plastic wrap and chill in refrigerator for 30 to 60 minutes or until dough is easy to handle

Nutrition facts per serving: 398 cal., 24 g total fat (12 g sat. fat), 135 mg chol., 191 mg sodium, 42 g carbo., 2 g fiber, 7 g pro. Daily values: 28% vit. A, 2% vit. C, 4% calcium, 19% iron

75

Express your style with your centerpiece—whether it's clean and simple, elegant and glittery, country fresh, or homespun traditional.

Apples and Roses

here's how...

1 Soak the floral foam in water, then cut the block in half. Center one half on each candle stand and push it onto the spike. To keep the floral foam from slipping, secure it to the candle stand with strips of floral tape or cellophane tape.

2 For each arrangement, attach three bunches of grapes to wooden florist's picks. Insert one bunch at each of two corners and insert the third bunch in the center of the opposite side.

3 Use florist's picks (snip the wire off) to secure apples to the floral foam. Place them to create a curving line across the front and back of the arrangement or diagonally across the floral foam.

4 Fill in around the apples with roses, cutting the stems so all the rose heads are at about the same height. At the rim of the candle stand, angle the flowers toward the table.

Whether you're hosting sit-down dinners or casual buffets, your dining table offers the perfect stage for holiday decorating. Keep the centerpiece low if you'll be seating guests around the table so they won't have to peer through flowers to converse. If you won't be using the table for dining, create an eye-catching display that imbues the whole room with a holiday feeling. If a single arrangement looks lonely, make two and place them symmetrically on each side of the center. Or make three to five small arrangements and place them along the length of the table.

SHOPPING LIST

2 footed candle
    stands with spikes
floral foam
waterproof floral tape
    or cellophane tape
wooden florist's picks
    with wires
red or green grapes
green apples
2 dozen white roses

rosy tip
■ Buy the roses a day or two ahead of the party and let them stand in room-temperature water. They'll be almost fully open when you're ready to arrange them.

five easy

centerpieces

Fruit Pyramid

From a floral-supply shop:
   floral foam
   wooden florist's picks
   boxwood clippings,
      myrtle sprigs, or other
      fresh evergreens
From a hardware store or
   garden shop:
      galvanized buckets in
      graduated sizes
From a grocery store:
   1 pineapple
   three kinds of fruit in
      graduated sizes, such
      as pears, lemons,
      and apples

here's how...

1 Pack each bucket full of floral foam. Stack the buckets, aligning the handles.

2 Secure the fruit to the floral foam with florist's picks, arranging them so all pieces point in the same direction. (This creates a pleasing rhythm that leads the eye around the design.) Crown the design with the pineapple, securing it with two florist's picks.

3 Tuck sprigs of boxwood or other evergreens between each piece of fruit to hide the floral foam and soften the edges of the buckets.

79

Boxwood Christmas Tree

here's how...

1 Soak the floral foam in water, then use a sharp knife to trim the block into a pyramidal tree shape. Wedge the block into the plastic container.

2 Starting at the bottom of the form and working toward the top, insert boxwood stems into the floral foam. Insert the lowest branches at a downward angle to hide the container. Gradually shorten the stem lengths as you work toward the top of the form and angle the stems at the top so they point up and out.

3 With the glue gun, glue apple slices, pepper berries, and ribbon bows to the boxwood. Loosely wrap grapevine around the tree and insert cinnamon sticks into the floral foam. Glue a cinnamon stick to the back of the snowman ornament, and push the stick into the top of the tree.

Paper Lanterns

here's how...

1 Enlarge the pattern by 550 percent (have a copy shop do this for you; it will require several passes on a copier). Or measure the circumference of your hurricane lantern and add 1 inch; measure the height and add 7 inches. Cut the paper to these measurements, and transfer the pattern to the paper.

2 Cut the paper along the solid lines indicated on the pattern. Fold along the dashed lines. Cut out the rectangular windows as shown. Use the paper punch to punch holes where indicated between the windows.

3 Use a pencil to curl the top and bottom strips.

4 Wrap the paper into a cylinder and fasten it along the edges with a stapler or double-stick tape. Slide the paper lantern over the hurricane lantern.

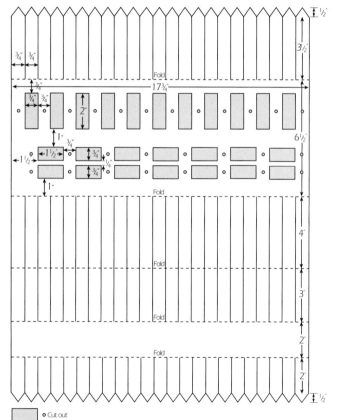

Cut out

Snowflakes and Lace

For a fresh and fun tablescape, cover your table with a red cloth, then scatter purchased paper snowflakes and doilies over the cloth. Top them with a layer of inexpensive tulle, which will keep the snowflakes in place. Add cut-paper slipcovers over hurricane lanterns for a touch of whimsy (see the instructions at left).

80

Served on a Platter

❧This centerpiece can be assembled at practically the last minute. Just place a silver serving tray (or use brass or glass, if you prefer) in the center of the table. Arrange pillar candles of different heights just off center. Place fresh fir, holly, and apples around the candles, extending the branches along the length of the tray. Insert a few stems of roses and lilies into florist's water vials (these are available from floral-supply shops and some crafts stores) and tuck the flowers among the apples and greenery. Unwind a coil of wired star garland and loop it around the arrangement in a free-form style (just be sure to keep it clear of the candle flames).

Few holidays are as firmly rooted in food traditions as Thanksgiving. Turkey, stuffing, and cranberries are just a few of the must-have dishes. While everyone has favorites associated with this feast, it's fun to put a new twist on the expected basics.

thanksgiving
mix and match

Make-Ahead Chived Mashed Potatoes

Mashed potatoes are a favorite at this time of year. And it's always a good idea to have at least a few dishes like this one that can be made ahead of the Thanksgiving cooking frenzy. The cream cheese and sour cream with chives make these mashed potatoes particularly rich and luscious.

- 9 medium potatoes (about 3 pounds)
- 1 8-ounce container sour cream dip with chives
- 1 3-ounce package cream cheese, cut up
- ¾ teaspoon onion salt
- ¼ teaspoon garlic salt
- ¼ teaspoon pepper
- ¼ to ½ cup milk
- 1 tablespoon butter or margarine
  Fresh whole chives (optional)

Peel and quarter potatoes. Cook, covered, in boiling salted water for 20 to 25 minutes or until tender. Drain potatoes. Mash potatoes with a potato masher or beat with an electric mixer on low speed.

Add sour cream dip, cream cheese, onion salt, garlic salt, and pepper. Gradually beat in enough of the milk to make smooth and fluffy. Turn into a greased 2-quart casserole. Cover and chill for up to 24 hours.

To serve, dot with butter or margarine. Bake, uncovered, in a 325° oven for 60 to 65 minutes or until potatoes are heated through. Garnish with whole chives, if desired. Makes 10 servings.

Nutrition facts per serving: 197 cal., 7 g total fat (3 g sat. fat), 13 mg chol., 348 mg sodium, 30 g carbo., 2 g fiber, 4 g pro. Daily values: 5% vit. A, 16% vit. C, 2% calcium, 3% iron

Trio of Fruits Salsa

When you want something more than traditional cranberry sauce, try this colorful relish that combines dried apricots and raisins with cranberries.

- 1½ cups chopped cranberries
- ⅓ cup snipped dried apricots
- ⅓ cup golden raisins
- ⅓ cup finely chopped green sweet pepper
- ¼ cup thinly sliced green onions (2)
- 1 tablespoon seeded and finely chopped fresh jalapeño pepper*
- ¼ cup sugar
- 3 tablespoons apricot nectar or orange juice
- 2 tablespoons salad oil
- 1 tablespoon snipped fresh cilantro
- ½ teaspoon grated fresh gingerroot
- ¼ teaspoon salt

Stir together cranberries, apricots, raisins, sweet pepper, green onions, and jalapeño pepper in a large mixing bowl. Add the sugar and toss gently to mix.

Combine the apricot nectar, salad oil, cilantro, ginger, and salt in a screw-top jar. Cover and shake well. Pour over cranberry mixture, tossing gently to coat. Cover and chill for 2 to 24 hours, stirring occasionally.

Let stand at room temperature for 30 minutes before serving. Serve as an accompaniment to sliced turkey or roast beef, if desired. Makes about 2½ cups (10 servings).

*Note: Hot peppers contain oils that can burn eyes, lips, and sensitive skin. Wear plastic gloves while preparing peppers and be sure to thoroughly wash your hands afterward.

Nutrition facts per tablespoon: 21 cal., 1 g total fat (0 g sat. fat), 0 mg chol., 14 mg sodium, 4 g carbo., 0 g fiber, 0 g pro. Daily values: 1% vit. A, 5% vit. C, 0% calcium, 0% iron

Trio of Fruits Salsa

Fruity Waldorf Salad

Kiwifruit and pineapple add a refreshing zing of color and flavor to the more expected apple, walnuts, and celery.

> 1 20-ounce can pineapple chunks (juice pack), drained (2 cups)
> 1 large apple or pear, cored and coarsely chopped (1½ cups)
> ½ cup thinly sliced celery
> ½ cup halved seedless red grapes
> ⅓ cup walnut pieces, toasted
> ¼ cup mayonnaise or salad dressing
> ¼ cup dairy sour cream

> 2 kiwifruit, peeled, halved lengthwise, and sliced (½ cup)
> Lettuce leaves (optional)

Toss together pineapple, apple or pear, celery, grapes, and walnuts in a large bowl. For dressing, stir together the mayonnaise or salad dressing and sour cream in a small bowl; gently fold into fruit mixture.

Cover and chill for 2 to 24 hours. Just before serving, stir in kiwifruit slices. Serve on lettuce leaves, if desired. Makes 8 servings.

Nutrition facts per serving: 170 cal., 10 g total fat (2 g sat. fat), 7 mg chol., 52 mg sodium, 20 g carbo., 1 g fiber, 2 g pro. Daily values: 3% vit. A, 50% vit. C, 3% calcium, 3% iron

Glazed Roasted Vegetables

Mixed Green Salad with Tomato-Basil Vinaigrette

- 2 cups torn spinach
- 1 cup torn Boston or Bibb lettuce
- 1 cup torn red-tip leaf lettuce
- 1 cup watercress
- 1 cup sliced fresh mushrooms
  Tomato-Basil Vinaigrette (see recipe, page 85)

Combine spinach, Boston or Bibb lettuce, and red-tip leaf lettuce in a large mixing bowl. Divide greens among 4 salad plates. Top each salad with watercress and mushrooms. Drizzle

Glazed Roasted Vegetables

At the end of roasting, increase the oven temperature to caramelize the brown sugar.

- 8 medium carrots, bias-sliced 1 inch thick (4 cups)
- 4 medium parsnips, bias-sliced 1 inch thick (4 cups)
- 12 baby beets, peeled and halved, or 3 small whole beets, quartered (about 12 ounces)
- 2 tablespoons snipped fresh parsley
- 2 teaspoons snipped fresh marjoram, thyme, or rosemary, or ½ teaspoon dried marjoram, thyme, or rosemary, crushed
- ¼ teaspoon salt
- 3 tablespoons olive oil or cooking oil
- 4 cups peeled, seeded winter squash cut into 1½-inch pieces (about 2 pounds before trimming)
- ¼ cup packed brown sugar

Cook carrots and parsnips, covered, in a small amount of boiling water in a large saucepan for 3 minutes. Drain.
Combine the partially cooked carrots and parsnips and the beets in a 13×9×2-inch baking pan. Sprinkle with parsley; marjoram, thyme, or rosemary; and salt. Drizzle with oil. Toss gently to coat vegetables. Cover the pan with foil.
Bake in a 375° oven for 30 minutes, stirring vegetables once. Stir in winter squash pieces. Cover and bake about 20 minutes more or just until vegetables are barely done. Remove vegetables from oven.
Increase oven temperature to 450°. Stir the brown sugar into vegetables until mixed. Return vegetables to oven and bake, uncovered, 15 to 20 minutes more or until vegetables are tender and glazed. Transfer to a serving dish. Makes 8 to 10 side-dish servings.

Nutrition facts per serving: 155 cal., 4 g total fat (1 g sat. fat), 0 mg chol., 112 mg sodium, 29 g carbo., 7 g fiber, 2 g pro. Daily values: 170% vit. A, 31% vit. C, 5% calcium, 8% iron

stuffing safety tips

■ Handling: Always wash your hands, work surfaces, and utensils in hot soapy water after handling raw poultry to prevent spreading bacteria to other foods.

■ Stuff just before roasting: Do not stuff the turkey until you are ready to roast it. Allow about ¾ cup stuffing for each pound of ready-to-cook turkey.

■ Don't stuff too tightly: When spooning the stuffing into the turkey cavity, do not overpack, as it may prevent the stuffing from cooking to a safe temperature.

■ Check the temperature: The stuffing in a bird should register at least 165° when a meat thermometer is inserted in the thickest part of the stuffing.

■ Serving: Serve poultry and stuffing immediately after cooking, and refrigerate any leftovers as soon as possible.

Tomato-Basil Vinaigrette over each salad. Makes 4 servings.

TOMATO-BASIL VINAIGRETTE:
Combine 1 large tomato, peeled, seeded, and cut up (¾ cup); 3 tablespoons salad oil; 3 tablespoons red wine vinegar; 2 tablespoons snipped fresh basil or 1½ teaspoons dried basil, crushed; ½ teaspoon sugar; ¼ teaspoon prepared horseradish; ⅛ teaspoon pepper; and 1 clove garlic, minced, in a food processor bowl or blender container. Cover and process or blend until smooth. Makes about ¾ cup.

Nutrition facts per salad with dressing: 117 cal., 11 g total fat (2 g sat. fat), 0 mg chol., 35 mg sodium, 6 g carbo., 2 g fiber, 2 g pro. Daily values: 28% vit. A, 38% vit. C, 4% calcium, 9% iron

Golden Wild Rice Stuffing

For a change from traditional bread stuffing, tuck this rice mixture into the turkey cavity before roasting. Or serve the stuffing right after it's cooked.

½ cup wild rice
½ cup regular brown rice
1 14½-ounce can chicken broth
½ cup water
1 to 1½ teaspoons poultry seasoning or ½ to 1 teaspoon ground sage
1 cup shredded parsnip
1 cup shredded carrot
1 cup chopped celery
1 cup chopped onion
2 tablespoons snipped fresh parsley
½ teaspoon salt

Rinse wild rice in a strainer under cold running water. In a 3-quart saucepan combine rices, broth, water, and poultry seasoning or sage.
Bring to boiling; reduce heat. Cover and simmer for 35 minutes. Add vegetables, parsley, and salt. Simmer,

covered, for 15 minutes or until vegetables are tender, stirring often. Use to stuff one 8- to 10-pound turkey or serve immediately. Makes 10 servings.

Nutrition facts per serving: 95 cal., 1 g total fat (0 g sat. fat), 0 mg chol., 257 mg sodium, 19 g carbo., 2 g fiber, 3 g pro. Daily values: 31% vit. A, 9% vit. C, 2% calcium, 4% iron

Pesto-Artichoke Stuffing

1 6-ounce package chicken-flavored stuffing mix
1 14½-ounce can chunky pasta-style tomatoes
¼ cup butter or margarine
3 tablespoons pesto
2 tablespoons water*

1 14-ounce can artichoke hearts, rinsed, drained, and chopped
¼ cup toasted pine nuts or chopped almonds

Combine seasoning packet from stuffing mix, undrained tomatoes, butter or margarine, pesto, and water in a 2-quart saucepan. Bring to boiling; add artichoke hearts. Reduce heat; cover and simmer for 6 minutes.
Remove saucepan from heat. Stir in stuffing mix and pine nuts. Cover and let stand for 5 minutes. Fluff with a fork before serving. Makes 5 cups (about 8 servings).
***Note:** For a moister stuffing, add 1 to 3 tablespoons more water after cooking.

Nutrition facts per serving: 233 cal., 13 g total fat (5 g sat. fat), 27 mg chol., 754 mg sodium, 25 g carbo., 1 g fiber, 6 g pro. Daily values: 11% vit. A, 14% vit. C, 4% calcium, 11% iron

85

Pesto-Artichoke Stuffing

For seven days, from December 26 to January 1, African-Americans celebrate their African heritage and affirm seven important principles of community and family life. As with most holidays, traditional foods play a central role.

kwanzaa

The seven principles of Kwanzaa are unity, self-determination, collective work and responsibility, cooperative economics, purpose, creativity, and faith. The colors of Kwanzaa—green, black, and red—often are visible on the holiday table, along with the symbolic elements (see page 88). Serve these African-inspired foods during your celebration.

African-Creole Turkey Gumbo

For convenience, use 1½ teaspoons Cajun seasoning in place of the crushed red pepper, paprika, thyme, black pepper, and ground red pepper.

  1 pound fresh or frozen medium shrimp, peeled and deveined
  3 cups fresh or frozen cut okra, thawed (12 ounces)
  2 tablespoons cooking oil
  1 tablespoon sugar
  1 tablespoon vinegar
  ⅔ cup all-purpose flour
  ½ cup cooking oil
  ½ cup chopped onion
  ¼ cup chopped celery
  ¼ cup chopped green sweet pepper
  1 clove garlic, minced
  ¼ teaspoon crushed red pepper
  ¼ teaspoon paprika
  ¼ teaspoon dried thyme, crushed
  ¼ teaspoon black pepper
  ⅛ teaspoon ground red pepper
  4 cups reduced-sodium chicken broth
  ⅓ cup tomato paste
  1 bay leaf
  6 ounces cooked andouille or smoked sausage, halved lengthwise and cut into ½-inch-thick slices
  1 cup chopped cooked turkey or chicken
  4 ounces cooked crabmeat, cut into bite-sized pieces (optional)
  1 tablespoon creamy peanut butter
  ¾ teaspoon filé powder (gumbo filé)
  5 cups hot cooked rice
    Bottled hot pepper sauce
    Fresh marjoram sprigs (optional)

Thaw shrimp, if frozen. Rinse shrimp and pat dry; set aside.

Cook okra in the 2 tablespoons oil and sugar in a saucepan about 8 minutes or until almost tender. Remove from heat; stir in vinegar and set aside.

For roux, stir together flour and the ½ cup oil in a heavy 4-quart Dutch oven until smooth. Cook over medium-high heat for 5 minutes, stirring constantly with a long-handled wooden spoon. Reduce heat to medium. Cook and stir constantly 10 to 15 minutes more or until roux is a dark reddish-brown. Stir in onion, celery, green pepper, garlic, crushed red pepper, paprika, thyme, black pepper, and ground red pepper (or Cajun seasoning, if using). Cook and stir over medium heat about 5 minutes or until vegetables are tender.

Gradually stir broth into roux mixture. Stir in tomato paste and bay leaf. Bring mixture to boiling. Add shrimp. Cook 2 minutes or until shrimp turn opaque. Stir in sausage, turkey, crabmeat (if using), cooked okra, peanut butter, and filé powder. Heat through. Discard bay leaf. Season to taste with salt and pepper. Serve over hot cooked rice. Pass hot pepper sauce. Garnish with fresh marjoram sprigs, if desired. Makes 10 servings.

Nutrition facts per serving: 415 cal., 22 g total fat (5 g sat. fat), 77 mg chol., 501 mg sodium, 37 g carbo., 2 g fiber, 18 g pro. Daily values: 9% vit. A, 25% vit. C, 5% calcium, 22% iron

Corn Sticks (see recipe, page 88)

African-Creole Turkey Gumbo

87

Corn Sticks

*If using only one corn stick pan, you may
need to refrigerate batter and grease pan
between batches (see photo, page 87).*

    1   cup all-purpose flour
    1   cup yellow cornmeal
    2 to 4 tablespoons sugar
    1   tablespoon baking powder
    ½   teaspoon salt
    2   beaten eggs
    1   cup milk
    ¼   cup cooking oil or
        shortening, melted

Grease a pan having 6 to 8 corn stick
shapes (or twelve 2½-inch muffin
cups); set aside.

Stir together the flour, cornmeal,
sugar, baking powder, and salt in a
medium mixing bowl. Make a well in
the center of the dry mixture; set aside.

Combine the eggs, milk, and cooking
oil or melted shortening in another
bowl. Add egg mixture all at once to dry
mixture. Spoon batter into the prepared
pans, filling pans ⅔ full.

Bake in a 425° oven for 12 to
15 minutes or until brown. Makes
24 to 26 corn sticks or 12 muffins.

Nutrition facts per corn stick: 74 cal., 3 g total fat
(1 g sat. fat), 19 mg chol., 100 mg sodium,
10 g carbo., 0 g fiber, 2 g pro. Daily values:
1% vit. A, 0% vit. C, 4% calcium, 3% iron

Beef and Groundnut Stew

    1½ pounds boneless beef chuck
        pot roast, cut into 1-inch
        cubes
    1   tablespoon peanut oil
        or cooking oil
    1   large onion, chopped (1 cup)
    2   cups water
    2   large tomatoes, peeled and
        chopped (1½ cups)

    ½   cup finely chopped fresh, mild
        green chili peppers (such as
        Anaheim)
        (see Note, page 83)
    ½   teaspoon salt
    ½   teaspoon crushed red pepper
    ¾   cup peanut butter
    3   cups hot cooked rice
    6   hard-cooked eggs,
        sliced (optional)

Trim fat from meat. In a 4-quart
Dutch oven brown half the beef in the
hot oil. Remove from pan. Brown
remaining beef with the onion, adding
more oil if necessary. Drain off fat.
Return all beef to pan.

Stir in water, tomatoes, chili peppers,
salt, and crushed red pepper. Bring to
boiling; reduce heat. Simmer, covered,
about 1½ hours or until meat is tender.

Remove about 1 cup of the broth
from the meat mixture; stir into peanut
butter. Return peanut butter mixture to
Dutch oven. Heat through. Serve over
hot cooked rice. Garnish with egg
slices, if desired. Makes 6 servings.

Nutrition facts per serving: 525 cal., 27 g total fat
(7 g sat. fat), 82 mg chol., 395 mg sodium,
35 g carbo., 3 g fiber, 38 g pro. Daily values:
5% vit. A, 69% vit. C, 3% calcium, 33% iron

Collard Greens with Coconut Milk

*Long a staple of soul food, collard greens
taste like a cross between cabbage
and kale. The addition of coconut milk
adds an exotic hint of intrigue to this
Southern favorite.*

    1   pound collard greens
    ¾   cup water
    ½   cup chopped onion
    1   cup light coconut milk or
        coconut milk
    ¼   teaspoon salt
    ¼   teaspoon pepper
    1   large tomato, seeded
        and chopped

Wash collard greens well. Remove
and discard stems; cut up leaves
(should have about 14 cups).

Bring water to boiling in a large pan
or Dutch oven. Add collard greens and
onion. Return to boiling; reduce heat.
Simmer, covered, for 10 minutes. Drain
well and return to pan.

Stir in coconut milk, salt, and
pepper. Cook, uncovered, over
medium-low heat for 10 minutes more
or until slightly thickened. Stir in
tomatoes; heat through. Serve
immediately. Makes 6 to 8 servings.

Nutrition facts per serving: 57 cal., 2 g total fat
(1 g sat. fat), 0 mg chol., 117 mg sodium,
9 g carbo., 3 g fiber, 2 g pro. Daily values:
25% vit. A, 27% vit. C, 2% calcium, 4% iron

symbolic elements of the kwanzaa table

■ Mkeka: a straw mat
representing tradition as the
foundation on which everything
else rests.

■ Kinara: a seven-branched
candleholder symbolizing the
ancestors. A candle is lit each day.

■ Mshumaa: the seven candles
representing the principles that are
the focus of the celebration.

■ Muhindi: ears of corn, standing
for the children, or potential for
children, and hence posterity.

■ Kikombe cha umoja: the unity
cup that is passed from guest to
guest filled with a libation to
honor the ancestors.

■ Zawadi: small gifts that reward
personal achievement.

Pinto Beans and Rice

Put ham, beans, and rice together and you've got a hearty, spicy starch dish. If you like, serve smaller portions to accompany meat.

 1¼ cups dry pinto beans (8 ounces)
 1 medium onion, chopped (½ cup)
 2 cloves garlic, minced
 1 bay leaf
 ½ teaspoon dried thyme, crushed
 ½ teaspoon pepper
 2 small smoked ham hocks (about 8 ounces each)
 8 ounces cooked smoked sausage, cut into ¾-inch pieces
 ¼ teaspoon salt
 3 cups hot cooked rice

Rinse beans. Combine beans and 3 cups water in a large saucepan. Bring to boiling; reduce heat. Simmer for 2 minutes. Remove from heat. Cover and let stand for 1 hour.

Drain beans and return to saucepan. Add onion, garlic, bay leaf, thyme, pepper, and 3 cups fresh water. Add ham hocks. Heat to boiling; reduce heat. Cover and simmer 1½ to 2 hours or until beans are tender, adding more water if necessary and stirring occasionally.

Remove ham hocks; cool slightly. Remove meat from ham hocks; chop meat and set aside. Discard bay leaf. Cook sausage in a medium skillet over medium heat about 5 minutes or until browned, stirring occasionally. Stir chopped meat, cooked sausage, and salt into beans. Cover and cook about 5 minutes more or until heated through. Serve over hot cooked rice. Makes 6 main-dish servings.

Nutrition facts per serving: 413 cal., 14 g total fat (5 g sat. fat), 38 mg chol., 943 mg sodium, 48 g carbo., 3 g fiber, 23 g pro. Daily values: 0% vit. A, 14% vit. C, 5% calcium, 28% iron

Sweet-Potato Biscuits

Self-rising flour contains baking powder and salt; however, the extra leavening added here makes these golden biscuits tender and very flaky.

 1 cup mashed, cooked sweet potato*
 ¼ cup sugar
 1 beaten egg
 1 cup milk
 3 cups self-rising flour
 1 teaspoon baking powder
 ½ cup shortening

Combine mashed sweet potato, sugar, and egg. Beat with a fork until smooth. Stir in milk. Set mixture aside.

Stir together flour and baking powder in a large mixing bowl. Cut in shortening until mixture resembles coarse crumbs. Make a well in the center of dry mixture. Add sweet-potato mixture and stir just until combined.

Turn out onto a well-floured surface. Knead gently for 10 to 12 strokes. Roll or pat dough to ½-inch thickness. Cut with a floured 2½-inch biscuit cutter. Reroll as necessary. Place biscuits 1 inch apart on large baking sheets.

Bake in a 400° oven for 12 to 15 minutes or until biscuits are lightly browned. Makes 18 to 20 biscuits.

***Note:** To make 1 cup mashed potatoes, peel 2 medium sweet potatoes (about 1 pound total). Cut into 1½-inch chunks. Place in a large amount of boiling water. Simmer about 20 minutes or until very tender. Drain. Mash with a potato masher or beat with an electric mixer.

Nutrition facts per biscuit: 165 cal., 6 g total fat (2 g sat. fat), 13 mg chol., 297 mg sodium, 23 g carbo., 3 g fiber, 3 g pro. Daily values: 32% vit. A, 5% vit. C, 9% calcium, 6% iron

Sweet-Potato Biscuits

Of all the festivals we celebrate, New Year's Eve is the oldest. Even the ancient civilizations of the Egyptians, Romans, and Druids greeted the new year by wearing masks, making lots of noise, and overindulging in food and drink.

new year's *through* the years

We owe the custom of celebrating New Year's Day on January 1 to Julius Caesar, who, as emperor in the first century B.C., devised the Julian calendar. In almost every country of the world, New Year's Eve is a time for feasting and fun, whether with a small group or a large gathering. Here is a selection of appetizers and beverages to help start your party planning.

Phyllo-Wrapped Brie with Mushrooms

1½ cups sliced fresh mushrooms
1   tablespoon butter or margarine
1   tablespoon snipped
      fresh parsley
1   tablespoon dry sherry
1   teaspoon Worcestershire sauce
¼   teaspoon dried thyme, crushed
      Dash pepper
4   sheets frozen phyllo dough
      (18×14-inch rectangles),
      thawed
3   tablespoons butter or
      margarine, melted
1   4½-inch round Brie cheese
      (8 ounces)
    Apple or pear wedges or
      unsalted crackers

Cook mushrooms in the 1 tablespoon butter in a medium skillet over medium heat until tender, stirring frequently. Stir in parsley, sherry, Worcestershire sauce, thyme, and pepper. Cook, uncovered, about 1 minute or until liquid evaporates. Remove from heat. Set aside to cool.

Lightly brush 1 sheet of phyllo dough with some of the 3 tablespoons melted butter or margarine. Place another sheet of phyllo dough on top of the first sheet and brush with butter. Repeat with 2 more sheets of phyllo, brushing each with butter. Cut an 11-inch circle from the stack. Discard trimmings.

Slice Brie in half horizontally. Place one half in center of phyllo stack. Spoon half the mushroom mixture over cheese. Top with other half of Brie and remaining mushroom mixture.

Wrap phyllo up and over Brie and mushrooms, pleating phyllo as needed to cover. Brush phyllo with remaining butter. Place in a shallow baking pan. **Bake in a 350° oven** for 20 to 25 minutes or until golden. Serve at once with apples, pears, or crackers. Makes 6 servings.

Nutrition facts per serving: 242 cal., 19 g total fat (11 g sat. fat), 58 mg chol., 397 mg sodium, 8 g carbo., 0 g fiber, 9 g pro. Daily values: 17% vit. A, 5% vit. C, 6% calcium, 7% iron

Italian Chicken Spirals

Italian Chicken Spirals

- 6 large skinless, boneless chicken breast halves (about 2 pounds total)
- 6 medium spinach leaves, stems removed
- 6 thin slices prosciutto (about 2½ ounces total)
- ½ cup mascarpone cheese or cream cheese, softened
- 1 tablespoon olive oil
- ¼ teaspoon paprika

  White and/or purple flowering kale (optional)

  Basil Mayonnaise

Place a chicken breast half, boned side up, between 2 pieces of plastic wrap. Pound chicken lightly to ¼-inch thickness. Repeat with remaining chicken breast halves. Set aside.

Place spinach leaves in a colander; pour boiling water over leaves in the colander set in sink. Drain spinach on paper towels.

Place a chicken breast half, smooth side down, on a cutting board or other flat surface. Season with salt and pepper. Arrange a slice of prosciutto on chicken. Spread a rounded tablespoon of cheese evenly over prosciutto. Arrange a spinach leaf on top.

Roll chicken tightly from one long edge and place, seam side down, in a greased shallow baking pan. Repeat with remaining chicken breast halves. Combine olive oil and paprika; brush over chicken.

Bake in a 375° oven for 25 to 30 minutes or until chicken is tender and no longer pink; cool slightly. Cover and refrigerate several hours.

To serve, trim off ends. Cut each chicken roll into 6 slices. Arrange slices on serving plate and garnish with kale, if desired. Serve with Basil Mayonnaise. Makes 36 appetizers.

BASIL MAYONNAISE: Place ¾ cup mayonnaise, ½ cup loosely packed fresh basil, ½ small shallot, and ½ clove garlic in a food processor bowl or blender container. Cover and process or blend until almost smooth. Cover and chill up to 4 hours. Serve in a sweet pepper half and garnish with fresh basil, if desired.

Nutrition facts per appetizer with mayonnaise: 84 cal., 7 g total fat (2 g sat. fat), 20 mg chol., 75 mg sodium, 0 g carbo., 0 g fiber, 6 g pro. Daily values: 1% vit. A, 0% vit. C, 0% calcium, 1% iron

Crostini with Olives and Feta Spread

Crostini with Olives and Feta Spread

1 loaf baguette-style French bread
½ of an 8-ounce jar oil-packed dried tomatoes
¼ cup chopped pitted Kalamata or ripe olives
1 clove garlic, minced
1 3-ounce package cream cheese
4 ounces feta or goat cheese, crumbled (1 cup)
2 tablespoons milk
  Shredded fresh basil leaves

For crostini, partially freeze bread. Cut forty ¼-inch-thick slices; arrange on baking sheets. Drain tomatoes, reserving oil. Lightly brush one side of each slice with some oil. Bake in a 300° oven 6 minutes. Turn slices over; bake 6 minutes or until golden brown. **Finely chop** tomatoes. Stir in olives and garlic. Set aside. Beat cream cheese in a small mixing bowl until softened. Beat in feta and milk until smooth. (If desired, cover both spreads; refrigerate up to 2 days. Bring to room temperature before spreading.) **Spread feta mixture** on oiled side of crostini. Top with a small dollop of tomato mixture. Garnish crostini with shredded basil. Makes 40 appetizers.

Nutrition facts per serving: 47 cal., 3 g total fat (2 g sat. fat), 8 mg chol., 124 mg sodium, 4 g carbo., 0 g fiber, 2 g pro. Daily values: 2% vit. A, 4% vit. C, 3% calcium, 1% iron

Mango-Kiwi Salsa with Jicama Chips

2 ripe mangoes, peeled and finely chopped
1 kiwifruit, peeled and finely chopped
1 green onion, thinly sliced (2 tablespoons)
¼ cup finely chopped red sweet pepper
1 teaspoon grated fresh gingerroot
1 tablespoon lime juice
1 tablespoon snipped fresh cilantro, parsley, or basil
1 tablespoon brown sugar
  Dash ground red pepper
1 medium jicama

For salsa, combine mango, kiwifruit, green onion, red sweet pepper, gingerroot, lime juice, cilantro, brown sugar, and ground red pepper in a mixing bowl. Toss to coat well. Cover and chill up to 4 hours. Makes about 2 cups salsa.

For jicama chips, peel and halve jicama. Cut jicama into ¼-inch-thick slices with a sharp knife. If desired, cut jicama slices into desired shapes using cookie cutters for the flower shapes shown on *page 93*. Serve with salsa.

Nutrition facts per tablespoon with jicama: 16 cal., 0 g total fat (0 g sat. fat), 0 mg chol., 0 mg sodium, 4 g carbo., 0 g fiber, 0 g pro. Daily values: 6% vit. A, 16% vit. C, 0% calcium, 0% iron

Black-Eyed Pea Hummus

In the South, black-eyed peas are eaten on New Year's Day to bring good luck. Here is a nontraditional approach to serving them: ground up in hummus in place of chickpeas.

1 15-ounce can black-eyed peas
½ cup tahini (sesame seed paste)
¼ cup snipped fresh cilantro
3 tablespoons lemon juice
3 tablespoons milk
2 tablespoons olive oil
½ teaspoon salt
¼ teaspoon ground cumin
2 cloves garlic, halved
  Toasted Pita Wedges and/or assorted crackers

Rinse and drain black-eyed peas; reserve a few in the refrigerator, covered, to use for garnish. Combine remaining black-eyed peas, tahini, cilantro, lemon juice, milk, olive oil, salt, cumin, and garlic in a large food processor bowl. Cover and process until mixture is smooth.

Transfer to a serving dish. Serve immediately or cover and chill for up to 24 hours. Before serving, garnish with reserved black-eyed peas. Serve with Toasted Pita Wedges and/or assorted crackers. Makes 1½ cups spread.

TOASTED PITA WEDGES: Split 4 small pita bread rounds; cut each half into 6 wedges. Place, cut sides up, on an ungreased baking sheet. Bake in a 375° oven 7 to 9 minutes or until lightly browned. Store in an airtight container.

Nutrition facts per tablespoon (without pita wedges or crackers): 61 cal., 4 g total fat (1 g sat. fat), 0 mg chol., 98 mg sodium, 5 g carbo., 1 g fiber, 2 g pro. Daily values: 0% vit. A, 2% vit. C, 1% calcium, 2% iron

Champagne Fruit Punch

Extend a bottle of champagne or sparkling wine by combining it with fruits and juices. Or make a no-alcohol version with pineapple juice.

1 16-ounce package frozen whole strawberries or unsweetened peach slices
¼ cup sugar
2½ cups orange juice
2 tablespoons lemon or lime juice
1 750-ml bottle champagne or sparkling wine or 4 cups unsweetened pineapple juice

Thaw fruit at room temperature but *do not drain*. Place fruit and juice in a food processor bowl or blender container. Add sugar. Cover and process or blend until smooth. To remove strawberry seeds, pour mixture through a fine sieve or a sieve lined with a double thickness of 100-percent-cotton cheesecloth.

Transfer pureed fruit to a 2-quart pitcher. Stir in orange juice and lemon or lime juice. (Punch can be prepared to this point, covered, and refrigerated overnight or until serving time.) Before serving, slowly stir in champagne, sparkling wine, or pineapple juice. Makes about 12 (5-ounce) servings.

Nutrition facts per serving: 94 cal., 0 g total fat (0 g sat. fat), 0 mg chol., 2 mg sodium, 14 g carbo., 1 g fiber, 1 g pro. Daily values: 1% vit. A, 67% vit. C, 0% calcium, 2% iron

Make-Believe Champagne

1 33.8-ounce bottle carbonated water, chilled
1 33.8-ounce bottle ginger ale, chilled
1 24-ounce bottle unsweetened white grape juice, chilled
  Party Ice Cubes

Combine chilled carbonated water, ginger ale, and grape juice in a large pitcher. Pour over ice cubes in chilled champagne glasses or wine glasses. Serve immediately. Makes about 20 (4-ounce) servings.

PARTY ICE CUBES: Place small pieces of fruit (berries or tiny citrus wedges), small sprigs of fresh mint, or ½-inch strips of orange peel into the compartments of ice cube trays. Add enough water to fill, then freeze.

Nutrition facts per serving: 37 cal., 0 g total fat (0 g sat. fat), 0 mg chol., 14 mg sodium, 9 g carbo., 0 g fiber, 0 g pro. Daily values: 0% vit. A, 0% vit. C, 0% calcium, 1% iron

bubbly tips

No New Year's festivities are complete without a toast of something bubbly at midnight. Champagne is the traditional drink, but there are many other choices among the sparkling wines, as well as a selection of nonalcoholic drinks.

Champagne Safety: It's important to remember that anything bubbly is under pressure. Releasing that pressure, while still enjoying the satisfying pop as the cork comes out, takes a certain amount of skill.

■ The number one rule to safe champagne cork removal is to be sure your wine is well chilled and rested, as jostling before serving can cause nasty accidents.

■ Remove the foil and carefully undo the wires holding the cork in place.

■ Set the bottle down in an upright position and cover with a napkin or towel so the cork can't take off like a rocket. Twist the cork (napkin still in place) back and forth until it pops.

■ Pour gently into chilled tulip-shape glasses (which preserve the fizz) and toast away!

Nonalcoholic Alternatives: For those who are not indulging in champagne, make sure you have a selection of nonalcoholic alternatives. Drinks that come in wine-type bottles tend to make the experience more festive, and some sparkling ciders and fruit spritzers even have a cork. Or try the Make-Believe Champagne recipe, at left.

93

Mango-Kiwi Salsa with Jicama Chips

Create a street full of cookie house fronts. Give them as gifts, creating a house style to match the recipient's home, or choose one style for all the cookies you decorate. Throw a party and invite friends to trim houses to match their own homes.

cookie boulevard

Prepare either or both of the cookie doughs, depending on how many cookie houses you want to bake and whether you want dark- or light-colored houses. While the dough chills, make pattern(s); follow directions on page 97.

Gingerbread Cookie Dough

One batch of dough is enough to make about 4 house fronts (or 3 house fronts and several details). If you want to make additional cookie houses, prepare separate batches of dough. A double recipe is too much for most large mixing bowls.

½ cup shortening
½ cup sugar
1 teaspoon baking powder
1 teaspoon ground ginger
½ teaspoon baking soda
½ teaspoon ground cinnamon
½ teaspoon ground cloves
½ cup molasses
1 egg
1 tablespoon vinegar
2½ cups all-purpose flour

Beat shortening in a large mixing

bowl with an electric mixer on medium to high speed for 30 seconds. Add sugar, baking powder, ginger, baking soda, cinnamon, and cloves; beat until combined, scraping sides of bowl occasionally. Beat in molasses, egg, and vinegar until combined. Beat in as much of the flour as you can with the mixer. Stir in any remaining flour with a wooden spoon. Cover and chill about 3 hours or until dough is easy to handle. Roll out, cut, and bake as directed.

***Note**—To make Gingerbread Cookies instead of house fronts from dough: Prepare dough and roll half at a

Southwestern

time to ⅛-inch thickness on a lightly floured surface. Using a 2½-inch cookie cutter, cut into desired shapes. Place 1 inch apart on a greased cookie sheet. Bake in a 375° oven for 5 to 6 minutes or until edges are lightly browned. Cool on cookie sheet 1 minute. Transfer cookies to a wire rack; cool. If desired, frost cookies. Makes 36 to 48 cookies.

Nutrition facts per cutout cookie: 79 cal., 3 g total fat (1 g sat. fat), 6 mg chol., 30 mg sodium, 12 g carbo., 0 g fiber, 1 g pro. Daily values: 0% vit. A, 0% vit. C, 1% calcium, 4% iron

4

Victorian

Suburban ranch

Tudor

Sugar Cookie Dough

One batch of dough will make about 3 house fronts (or 2 house fronts and several details). If you want to make additional cookie houses, prepare separate batches of cookie dough.

- ⅓ cup butter, softened
- ⅓ cup shortening
- ¾ cup sugar
- 1 teaspoon baking powder
  Dash salt
- 1 egg
- 1 teaspoon vanilla
- 2 cups all-purpose flour

Beat butter and shortening in a medium mixing bowl with an electric mixer on medium to high speed for 30 seconds. Add sugar, baking powder, and salt; beat until combined, scraping sides of bowl occasionally. Beat in egg

and vanilla until combined. Beat in as much of the flour as you can with the mixer. Stir in any remaining flour with a wooden spoon. If necessary, cover and chill dough about 3 hours or until dough is easy to handle. Roll out, cut, and bake as directed.

*Note—To make Sugar Cookie Cutouts instead of house fronts from dough: Prepare dough and roll half of the dough at a time to ⅛-inch thickness on a lightly floured surface. Using a 2½-inch cookie cutter, cut into desired shapes. Place on ungreased cookie sheet. Bake in a 375° oven for 7 to 8 minutes or until edges are firm and bottoms are very lightly browned. Transfer cookies to a wire rack and let cool. If desired, frost cookies. Makes 36 to 48 cookies.

Nutrition facts per cutout cookie: 74 cal., 4 g total fat, (2 g sat. fat), 10 mg chol., 33 mg sodium, 9 g carbo., 0 g fiber, 1 g pro. Daily values: 1% vit. A, 0% vit. C, 1% calcium, 2% iron

Royal Icing

- 3 tablespoons meringue powder
- ⅓ cup warm water
- 1 16-ounce package powdered sugar, sifted (4½ cups)
- 1 teaspoon vanilla
- ½ teaspoon cream of tartar
  Paste food coloring

Combine meringue powder, water, powdered sugar, vanilla, and cream of tartar in a small mixing bowl. Beat with an electric mixer on low speed until combined, then on high speed for 7 to 10 minutes or until very stiff. Use the icing immediately.

Divide icing; tint with paste food coloring as desired. When not using icing, keep it covered with plastic wrap to prevent it from drying out. Store in refrigerator. Makes about 3 cups.

96

Georgian

Farmhouse

Cape Cod colonial

cookie house fronts

here's how...

1 Make a sketch of the house you want to duplicate, using a photo. Or use a copying machine to enlarge or shrink a photo to about 6 to 7 inches tall. Simplify small details, but keep those that characterize the house. For example, omit siding and gutter details, but include the style of a door, shutters, and special trim. Alternatively, copy one of the house styles shown here or enlarge the Victorian House pattern *below*.

2 Check supermarkets and bulk candy stores for lots of colorful decorating possibilities—cookies, pretzels, candies, gum, and nuts.

3 Prepare desired dough(s). Cover and chill while preparing patterns.

4 To make patterns, trace house shapes onto graph paper. Make 2 copies for each house. From one pattern, cut out details that you want to add dimension to the house, such as dormers, a roof, or a front porch. If desired, cover pattern pieces with clear self-adhesive shelf paper to make them more durable.

5 Lightly grease the back of a 15×10×1-inch baking pan. Roll some of the dough to ¼-inch thickness on the greased pan. Place some of the pattern pieces 1 inch apart on dough. Cut around piece with a sharp knife, as shown. Remove excess dough (save for

YOU'LL NEED:
several recipes Gingerbread Cookie Dough and/or Sugar Cookie Dough
graph paper
clear self-adhesive shelf paper (optional)
Royal Icing
pastry bags, couplers, and assorted tips (small round, star, zigzag)
waxed paper (optional)
assorted candies, candy-coated gum, peanuts, cookies, and pretzels

rerolling). Leave dough cutouts on the pan and bake in a 375° oven for 10 to 12 minutes or until edges are browned.

6 Place pattern pieces on the warm, baked cookie pieces and trim edges. Cool 3 minutes on pan. Loosen cookie pieces with a spatula. When completely cool, transfer to a wire rack. Repeat with remaining dough and patterns.

7 To decorate, prepare the Royal Icing. Divide and tint icing as desired, using paste food coloring. Fit pastry

bags with couplers and tips. Fill bags with icing, keeping any remaining icing covered with plastic wrap; refrigerate until needed. If desired, place cookie cutouts on waxed paper. Decorate as desired, piping on windows, doors, trim, and other elements as shown. Use icing to attach candies, other cookie cutouts, and edible garnishes. (If icing in bag begins to dry and plugs the decorating tip, just wipe tip with a clean wet cloth.) Use the house front photos on these pages for decorating ideas. Allow decorated cookies to dry about 2 hours.

97

PATTERN FOR VICTORIAN HOUSE

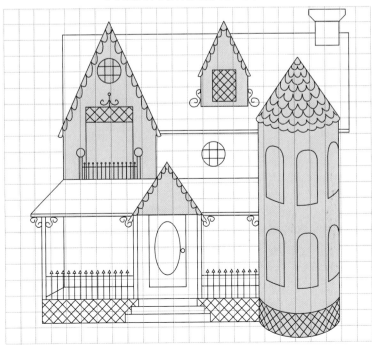

1 SQUARE = ABOUT ⅜ INCH

Christmas is the ideal time to go all out with fancy cookies and whimsical baking projects. Bring out the cookie cutters, decorative candies, colored sugars, and frostings. This is your chance to turn tasty cookies into creative treats.

creative *cookies*

Take ropes of cookie dough and twirl them into jolly snowmen. Make stained-glass cookies with crushed candies. Turn low-fat meringue into delicate angels. Or turn basic sugar cookies into festive ornaments.

Spiral Snowmen

These festive cookies are easy to shape and will delight children of all ages. Trim them simply if you like or decorate with frosting and gumdrop hats.

> ¾ cup butter, softened
> ¾ cup granulated sugar
> ¼ teaspoon baking powder
> 1 egg
> 1 teaspoon vanilla
> 2 cups all-purpose flour
>   Pearl sugar or coarse
>   granulated sugar (optional)
>   Red cinnamon candies,
>   miniature semisweet
>   chocolate pieces, and black
>   writing gel
>   Gumdrop Hats (optional)

Beat butter in a large mixing bowl with an electric mixer on medium to high speed for 30 seconds. Add granulated sugar and baking powder; beat until combined. Beat in egg and vanilla until combined. Beat in as much of the flour as you can with mixer. Stir in any remaining flour with a wooden spoon. Cover and chill dough about 30 minutes or until easy to handle.

Roll about 1½ tablespoons of the dough on a lightly floured surface into a 10-inch rope. On an ungreased cookie sheet, coil one end of the rope into a circle to make the head. Coil the other end of the rope in the opposite direction for the body (as shown). Repeat with remaining dough, placing cookies about 2 inches apart.

Sprinkle with pearl or coarse sugar, if desired. Add cinnamon candies for buttons and chocolate pieces for eyes.

Bake in a 375° oven for 10 to 12 minutes or until lightly browned. Let cookies cool 1 minute on cookie sheet. Remove cookies and cool completely on wire racks. Pipe on mouths with writing gel and attach Gumdrop Hats, if desired. Makes about 24 cookies.

GUMDROP HATS: For each hat, roll a large gumdrop in sugar into an oval. Roll oval into a cone shape; press to seal ends. Curl up bottom edge of cone to form a brim. Attach hat to head of snowman with frosting, if desired.

Nutrition facts per cookie: 113 cal., 6 g total fat (4 g sat. fat), 24 mg chol., 65 mg sodium, 14 g carbo., 0 g fiber, 1 g pro. Daily values: 5% vit. A, 0% vit. C, 0% calcium, 3% iron

here's how...

Spiral Snowmen – Coil ropes of dough into double spirals (as shown). Use a little more of the rope for the bottom of the snowman.

3

Chosolate Stars

Melted candy cane in each cookie's center gives the effect of stained glass and adds to the minty flavor of these confections.

- ⅔ cup shortening
- ½ cup sugar
- 1 teaspoon baking soda
- ½ teaspoon baking powder
- ¼ teaspoon salt
- ½ cup dark-colored corn syrup
- 1 egg
- ¼ cup milk
- ½ teaspoon mint extract
- ½ cup unsweetened cocoa powder
- 3 cups all-purpose flour
- 4 ounces candy canes, crushed (about ⅔ cup crushed)

Beat shortening in a large mixing bowl with an electric mixer on medium to high speed for 30 seconds. Add sugar, baking soda, baking powder, and salt; beat until combined. Beat in corn syrup, egg, milk, and mint extract until combined. Beat in cocoa powder and as much of the flour as you can with the mixer. Stir in any remaining flour with a wooden spoon.

Divide dough into 3 portions. Cover and chill about 1 hour or until dough is easy to handle.

Roll each portion of dough on a lightly floured surface to ⅛- to ¼-inch thickness. Cut with star-shaped cookie cutters. Place cutout dough on a foil-lined cookie sheet. Cut a small shape out of cookie centers. Fill center cutout with some crushed candy (as shown).

Bake in a 375° oven for 5 to 7 minutes or until slightly puffed and set. Cool cookies on foil; peel off foil and store cookies tightly covered. Makes about 48 cookies.

Nutrition facts per cookie: 85 cal., 3 g total fat (1 g sat. fat), 5 mg chol., 46 mg sodium, 13 g carbo., 0 g fiber, 1 g pro. Daily values: 0% vit. A, 0% vit. C, 1% calcium, 4% iron

Chocolate Stars

Spiral Snowmen

Meringue Angels
(see recipe, page 100)

Shortbread Trees
(see recipe, page 100)

Stamped Honey Cookies
(see recipe, page 100)

99

here's how...

Chocolate Stars – Spoon crushed candy canes (green and white, red and white, or multicolored candies) into the cutout centers before baking (as shown). After baking and cooling, peel cookies off of the foil. The candy will have melted during baking, giving the cookie a stained glass appearance.

Meringue Powder Glaze

This frosting makes a firm and flat coating on cookies. Use it as the smooth base for the sponge-painted and snowflake cookies (see photos, page 101). Look for meringue powder where cake decorating supplies are sold—it's different from powdered egg whites.

- 2 tablespoons meringue powder
- ¼ cup warm water
- 3½ cups sifted powdered sugar

Beat together meringue powder, water, and 2 cups of the sifted powdered sugar until smooth, using a fork. Gradually stir in the remaining powdered sugar to make a smooth glaze that is spreadable but not runny. (It should have a flowing consistency and be too thin to hold ridges when spread.) Makes about 1 cup glaze.

Stamped Honey Cookies

To retain the stamped design after baking, use a cookie recipe with little or no leavening (see photo, page 99).

- 1 cup butter, softened
- ⅔ cup sugar
- 1 egg
- 2 tablespoons honey
- 1 teaspoon vanilla
- 2½ cups all-purpose flour
- Powdered food coloring

Beat butter in a large mixing bowl with an electric mixer on medium to high speed for 30 seconds. Add the sugar and beat until combined. Beat in egg, honey, and vanilla until combined. Beat in as much of the flour as you can with the mixer. Stir in any remaining flour with a wooden spoon.

here's how...

Stamped Honey Cookies – Use a floured cookie stamp or the patterned bottom of a glass or dish to flatten the balls of dough. After baking, use a clean, small brush to add a light dusting of powdered food coloring, blotting off extra food coloring from the brush onto a paper towel. Brush the high parts of the stamped cookie (as shown).

Shape dough into 1- to 1½-inch balls. Place balls 2 inches apart on an ungreased cookie sheet. Using a floured cookie stamp or the floured patterned bottom of a glass or dish, flatten balls to ¼-inch thickness.

Bake in a 375° oven for 6 to 8 minutes or until bottoms are lightly browned. Cool on cookie sheet 1 minute. Remove cookies and cool on a wire rack. To decorate, brush cookies with powdered food coloring (as shown). Makes about 36 cookies.

Nutrition facts per cookie: 94 cal., 5 g total fat (3 g sat. fat), 20 mg chol., 54 mg sodium, 11 g carbo., 0 g fiber, 1 g pro. Daily values: 4% vit. A, 0% vit. C, 0% calcium, 2% iron

Shortbread Trees

See photo, page 99.

- 1¼ cups all-purpose flour
- 3 tablespoons sugar
- 3 tablespoons small multicolored nonpareils
- ½ cup butter
- Green food coloring
- Icing (optional)

here's how...

Shortbread Trees – Cut dough circle into 16 wedges with a long knife (as shown). After baking, recut the triangles and let cool on cookie sheet before completely cooling on wire racks. Drizzle with icing to look like garlands and decorate top of tree with a candy piece, if desired.

Miniature candy-coated chocolate pieces (optional)

Combine flour, sugar, and multicolored candies in a medium mixing bowl. Using a pastry blender, cut in butter until mixture resembles fine crumbs and starts to cling together. Form mixture into a ball and knead until smooth, working in enough food coloring to tint dough green.

Pat or roll dough into an 8-inch circle on an ungreased cookie sheet. Cut the circle into 16 pie-shaped wedges (as shown). Do not separate wedges.

Bake in a 325° oven for 25 to 30 minutes or until bottom just starts to brown and center is set. Cut the circle into wedges again while warm. Cool on the cookie sheet for 5 minutes. Remove cookies and cool on wire rack. Drizzle each tree with icing and add a chocolate piece to the top of the tree, if desired. Makes 16 cookies.

ICING: In a small bowl stir together ½ cup sifted powdered sugar, ½ teaspoon vanilla, and enough milk to make of drizzling consistency.

Nutrition facts per cookie: 103 cal., 6 g total fat (4 g sat. fat), 15 mg chol., 58 mg sodium, 11 g carbo., 0 g fiber, 1 g pro. Daily values: 5% vit. A, 0% vit. C, 0% calcium, 2% iron

Meringue Angels

Delicate meringues have the advantage of being delicious, low calorie, and low fat, a claim many other holiday cookies can't make (see photo, page 99).

- 2 egg whites
- ½ teaspoon vanilla
- ¼ teaspoon cream of tartar
- ½ cup sugar

Line a large cookie sheet with parchment paper or foil. Beat egg whites, vanilla, and cream of tartar until soft peaks form. Gradually add sugar, beating until stiff peaks form.

Put egg white mixture into a decorating bag fitted with a ¼-inch round tip, filling bag half full. Holding the decorating bag with the tip close to the parchment paper or foil, squeeze bag gently to form an angel with the egg white mixture (as shown). Repeat with the remaining meringue mixture.

Bake in a 300° oven about 8 minutes or until very light brown. Turn off oven and let cookies dry in the oven with the door closed for 15 to 20 minutes. After cooling, gently peel cookies off paper or foil. Makes about 24 cookies.

Nutrition facts per cookie: 18 cal., 0 g total fat (0 g sat. fat), 0 mg chol., 5 mg sodium, 4 g carbo., 0 g fiber, 0 g pro. Daily values: 0% vit. A, 0% vit. C, 0% calcium, 0% iron

here's how...

Meringue Angels – Pipe the meringue mixture onto parchment- or foil-lined cookie sheets so that cookies are easier to remove. Quickly make freehand outlines of the wings, body, and head (as shown). After baking and drying, gently peel the delicate meringue cookies off the paper or foil.

here's how...

Sponge-painted cookies – Prepare Sugar Cookie Dough (see recipe, page 96). Cut out shapes, bake, and cool cookies. Prepare Meringue Powder Glaze (see recipe, page 99) and spread tops of cookies with white glaze; let dry thoroughly. Using leftover glaze, thin for the "paint" with a little water and add desired food coloring (use paste food coloring for more intense colors). Crumple waxed paper and dip in the "paint." Dab on a paper towel to remove excess and then lightly dab on cookies (as shown). Let cookies dry.

here's how...

Snowflake cookies – Prepare Sugar Cookie Dough (see recipe, page 96). Cut out rounds using a fluted cookie cutter; bake and cool cookies. Prepare Meringue Powder Glaze (see recipe, page 99); divide glaze in half and tint half with food coloring. Working with one cookie at a time, spread top of cookie with white glaze. Place tinted glaze in a disposable pastry bag or plastic sandwich bag; cut off a small portion from tip, making a small opening. Immediately pipe contrasting colored icing in two concentric circles

plus a dot in center and several dots around edge. Drag toothpick from center dot to dots at edges (as shown).

here's how...

Cut and replace cookies – Prepare Sugar Cookie Dough (see recipe, page 96). Divide dough in half and tint each half with contrasting food coloring. Make cutouts and place on a cookie sheet. Using smaller cutouts, cut out the center of the cookies and replace center with contrasting colored dough (as shown).

here's how...

Snow-capped trees – Prepare Sugar Cookie Dough (see recipe, page 96), tinting dough with green food coloring. Cut out tree shapes with a cookie cutter. To decorate, melt 8 ounces vanilla-flavored candy coating over low heat. Stir in 2 tablespoons shortening for this amount of coating until shortening melts. Dip the top of the tree cutout in the coating mixture and let it drip down slightly (as shown). If desired, sprinkle with white pearl sugar or white nonpareils before coating sets.

Mix and match red and green plates, placemats, and napkins for a festive table setting. Buy inexpensive holiday-motif salad plates to layer over ordinary dinner plates or chargers (extra-large plates that rest under dinner plates). Tie an ornament to the napkin for a party-favor napkin ring.

In a Twinkling: Tabletops

◄ Toast the New Year with goblets temporarily embellished with self-adhesive gold stars from a stationer's or office-supply store. Simply peel the stars off when the party is over. Make party favors by dipping fortune cookies in melted chocolate. For each place setting, tie one cookie in a clear cellophane corsage bag (ask your florist to sell you a few bags, or check the candy-making section of a crafts store).

▲ Guide guests to their places with fresh-pear place cards. Decorate a blank card with a pear stamp, write each guest's name, and cut a slit in the top of the pear to hold the card.

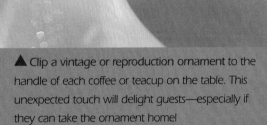

▲ Clip a vintage or reproduction ornament to the handle of each coffee or teacup on the table. This unexpected touch will delight guests—especially if they can take the ornament home!

▲ Give each place setting its own cheerful glow with a miniature candle clip. Look for reproduction candle clips, based on Victorian candleholders for trees, in mail order catalogs and Christmas shops. For a napkin ring, thread cranberries onto gold crafts wire and twist the wires together.

▶

String cranberries on fine gold crafts wire to make dainty bobèches for candles. Twist the wire ends together, then wrap the excess wire around a long nail to make fine curls.

Whether your parties are large or small, dress the chairs with slipcovers to create a festive mood.

special occasion seating

If your party plans exceed your seating capacity, don't despair. Diminutive tables, like the bistro tables shown on *page 105* can turn living room sofas and chairs into comfortable sit-down dining areas. Look for tables like these at chain home furnishings stores. Or use ordinary TV trays: dress them up by covering them with vintage dresser scarves or table runners.

Take advantage of unexpected spaces, too: an enclosed porch, for example, can become a dreamy temporary dining room. Layer inexpensive tulle and sheer organdy over porch chairs and a patio table *(above right)* to transform them for the occasion. Tuck a space heater in the corner to take any chill off the room. (For safety's sake, don't place the heater

close to the fabrics.) Keep the table decoration appropriately light and airy with frosty white ornaments and novelty candles resting on clear candlesticks of different heights.

For intimate dining or family meals, make the occasion special with holiday slipcovers (see *pages 106 and 107*). These tabard-style covers tie onto any chair back, and you can make them for Kwanzaa, Hanukkah, or Christmas— just choose fabric to reflect the holiday look you want to create.

Ballet Style

To dress your chairs with floor-length tutus *(below left)*, measure from the bottom of the chair leg up to the seat, across the seat to the back, up over the back, and down to the floor. For each chair, cut two or three pieces of 54- to 60-inch-wide tulle to that length and arrange them loosely over the chair. For the wrap that holds the dress in place, measure the width of the chair back and add about 6 inches.

Cut a piece of 54-inch-wide striped sheer organdy to that measurement. Fold under the raw edges and drape the fabric over the chair back, letting one selvage extend onto the chair seat and the other selvage fall to the back. Belt the fabric in place with wide ribbon at the middle of the chair back and with narrow ribbon just above the chair seat.

■ *Cover bistro tables or TV trays with lacy dresser scarves or fabric to create elegant individual dining tables.*

4

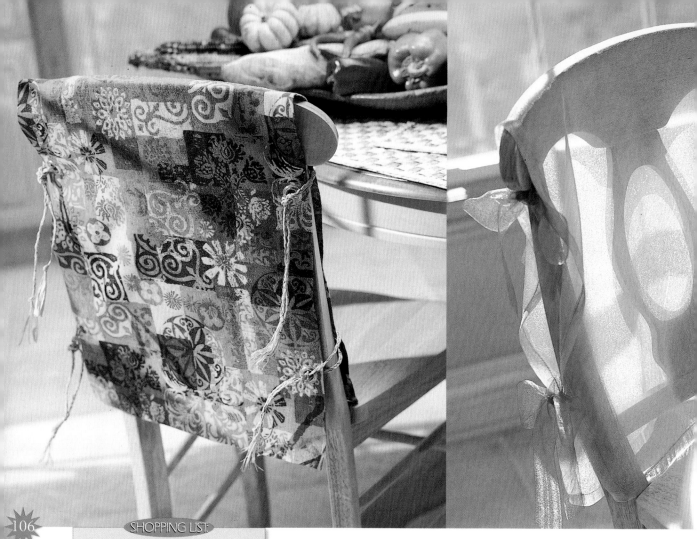

(For one chair slipcover)

FOR ALL STYLES:
  fabric (see the instructions at right to
  determine yardages)
  ¾-inch-wide paper-backed fusible
  web tape (optional)
For the eyelet-closure slipcover:
  extra-large eyelet kit, containing
  anvil, tool, eight eyelets, and eight
  washers (the eyelets have a ⅞-
  inch-diameter opening)
  hammer
  raffia
For the ribbon-closure slipcover:
  4 yards of 2-inch-wide
  sheer ribbon
For the frog-closure slipcover:
  fabric scraps
  four ⅞-inch-diameter black buttons
  4 yards of ¼-inch-diameter
  black cord
  hot-glue gun and glue sticks

here's how...

For all chair slipcovers

1 Measure the width of the chair
back, and add 3 inches for seam
allowances. Measure the chair back from
the bottom front, over the top, and down
to the bottom back. Add 3 inches for
seam allowances.

2 From the desired fabric, cut one
rectangle for each chair to be covered.
Note: Carefully consider the placement of
the fabric pattern on the slipcover front
and back. Allow for extra fabric to center
a large overall design or to match a plaid.

3 To machine-hem the slipcover:
Press under 1½ inches on each edge of
the fabric rectangle. Open up the pressed
fabric. Fold each raw edge to the pressed
edge, and finger-press in place. Refold
along the pressed edge, and press again

with an iron, setting both folds. Miter the
corners, if desired. Topstitch ½ inch from
the outer edge all around the rectangle.

4 For a no-sew hem: Press under 1½
inches on each edge of the fabric
rectangle. Open up the pressed fabric
and, following the manufacturer's
instructions, place the paper-backed
fusible web tape on the wrong side of the
fabric along the pressed edge. Fuse the
tape in place. Remove the paper backing
from the tape. Trim the hem even with
the fusible tape. Refold the hem and fuse.

For the eyelet closure

1 Follow the manufacturer's
instructions to install large eyelets. Gently
hammer the eyelets in pairs along the
side edges of the slipcover.

2 Use about six long strands of raffia
for each tie. Braid together three long
double strands of raffia until the tie is

about 24 inches long. Knot each end, leaving 2-inch tails to create tassel-like ends. Make a total of four braided ties.

3 Place the slipcover over the chair back. Lace the braided ties through the eyelets and tie the ends together in overhand knots.

For the ribbon closure

1 Cut eight 18-inch lengths of ribbon. **Press under a ⅜-inch seam allowance** at one short end of each ribbon. Pin the ribbons in pairs to the wrong side of the slipcover, matching the pressed short end with the edge of the hem. Topstitch in place. Place the slipcover over the chair back. Tie ribbons into bows.

For the frog closure

1 From fabric scraps, cut eight circles the size of the buttons.

2 Cut eight 18-inch lengths of black cord. On each length, find the center and slip a straight pin through the cord 1½ inches from the center on each side. The cord should now be marked with a 3-inch section in the center.

3 Roll the ends of each cord up to the pins, creating two flat spirals; let about ½ inch of the cord end extend from the center of the spiral (like a candlewick). Secure the spirals with straight pins. (See photo 3 *top right.*)

4 Apply hot glue over each spiral (on the side with the candlewick extending), cover with a fabric circle, and lightly press in place. (See photo 4, *center right*). After the glue sets, remove the pins.

5 To create the frogs, fold the spiraled lengths in half at the center, with the spirals touching and curling away from each other. Pin the frogs in pairs to

the right side of the slipcover front and back. (The spirals should just meet the topstitching.) Hot glue the spirals in place. Tack the cord at the stitching line.

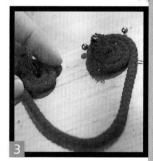

6 Stitch a button to the center of each loop on the front of the slipcover. (See photo 6, *below right*).

7 Place the slipcover over the chair back. Slip the buttons through the loops.

Nothing quite spells decadence the way chocolate does. Richly gracing a multitude of forms and flavors—in cakes, cookies, beverages, and mousses, with fruit, nuts, and liqueurs—chocolate is heavenly in all its incarnations.

have yourself a merry *chocolate* christmas

Chocolate Pots de Crème

Since this pudding dessert (poh duh KREM) is so rich, a small portion goes a long way. Spoon into tiny cups or dessert bowls. Then add a dollop of whipped cream to individual servings.

- 1 cup half-and-half or light cream
- 1 4-ounce package sweet baking chocolate, coarsely chopped
- 2 teaspoons sugar
- 3 beaten egg yolks
- ½ teaspoon vanilla

Combine cream, chocolate, and sugar in a heavy small saucepan. Cook and stir over medium heat for 10 minutes or until mixture reaches a full boil and thickens.

Gradually stir about *half* of the hot mixture into the beaten egg yolks. Stir egg yolk mixture into remaining hot mixture in pan. Cook and stir over low heat for 2 minutes more. Remove saucepan from heat.

Stir in vanilla until combined. Pour chocolate mixture into 4 to 6 pots de crème cups, demitasse cups, or small dessert bowls. Cover and chill for 2 to 24 hours. Makes 4 to 6 servings.

Nutrition facts per serving: 276 cal., 21 g total fat (11 g sat. fat), 182 mg chol., 31 mg sodium, 22 g carbo., 2 g fiber, 5 g pro. Daily values: 2% vit. A, 0% vit. C, 7% calcium, 7% iron

Chocolate-Raspberry Mousse Cake

When time is at a premium, dress up a cake mix with a mousse mix and ice cream topping. Although fresh raspberries may be costly at this time of year, you'll need only a few to decorate this simply elegant cake.

- 1 package 2-layer-size devil's food cake mix
- 2 2- to 2½-ounce packages chocolate mousse dessert mix

Chocolate-Raspberry Mousse Cake

⅔ cup cold milk
⅓ cup raspberry liqueur
1 11- to 12-ounce jar fudge ice cream topping or raspberry-fudge sauce
 Fresh raspberries
 Chocolate curls

Grease and lightly flour two 9×1½-inch round baking pans; set the baking pans aside.

Prepare, bake, and cool cake mix according to package directions.

Prepare mousse mixes according to package directions *except* use the ⅔ cup cold milk and the ⅓ cup liqueur for the total amount of liquid.

Split each cooled cake layer in half horizontally using a serrated knife. To assemble cake, place bottom of one split layer on a serving plate. Spread a thin layer of fudge topping (about ⅓ cup) over the bottom layer. Spread about ½ cup of the mousse mixture over the fudge topping. Repeat layering twice with cake, fudge topping, and

mousse mixture. Top with the remaining cake layer.

Frost top and sides with remaining mousse mixture. Before serving, decorate with fresh raspberries and chocolate curls. Store cake in the refrigerator. Makes 12 to 16 servings.

Nutrition facts per serving: 371 cal., 11 g total fat (4 g sat. fat), 2 mg chol., 464 mg sodium, 63 g carbo., 1 g fiber, 6 g pro. Daily values: 2% vit. A, 0% vit. C, 8% calcium, 14% iron

Berry Chocolate

Serve immediately with dippers; swirl as you dip. If the fondue mixture thickens, stir in some additional milk. Makes 8 servings.

Nutrition facts per serving (without dippers): 302 cal., 14 g total fat (9 g sat. fat), 18 mg chol., 72 mg sodium, 45 g carbo., 2 g fiber, 6 g pro. Daily values: 5% vit. A, 2% vit. C, 14% calcium, 7% iron

Yule Street Truffles

1 cup semisweet chocolate pieces
2 tablespoons butter
¼ cup sifted powdered sugar
1 tablespoon brandy
½ cup chopped toasted almonds
½ cup flaked coconut
½ cup whole pitted dates, chopped
¼ cup red candied cherries, chopped
8 ounces chocolate-flavored candy coating, melted
  Ground toasted almonds (optional)
  Sliced or slivered almonds (optional)
  Toasted flaked coconut (optional)
  Cocoa powder (optional)
  Melted chocolate and/or chocolate-flavored candy coating (optional)

Combine chocolate pieces and butter in a microwave-safe 1-quart casserole. Microcook, uncovered, on 100% power (high) for 1 to 2 minutes or until melted.

Stir in powdered sugar and brandy. Add chopped almonds, the ½ cup coconut, dates, and cherries. Shape mixture into ¾-inch balls. Dip in melted candy coating. Decorate with ground almonds, sliced or slivered almonds, toasted flaked coconut, cocoa

Berry Chocolate

1 ounce (2 tablespoons) chocolate liqueur
½ ounce (1 tablespoon) Chambord or other raspberry liqueur
1 cup prepared hot chocolate
  Whipped cream
  Chambord or other raspberry liqueur or unsweetened cocoa powder (optional)

Pour liqueurs into a 10-ounce mug. Add hot chocolate. Garnish with whipped cream; drizzle with a little Chambord or sprinkle with cocoa powder, if desired. Makes 1 serving.

Nutrition facts per serving: 345 cal., 5 g total fat (3 g sat. fat), 18 mg chol., 154 mg sodium, 48 g carbo., 1 g fiber, 9 g pro. Daily values: 15% vit. A, 3% vit. C, 24% calcium, 0% iron

Chocolate Fondue

For a mocha-flavored fondue, substitute ½ cup strong brewed coffee for the milk.

8 ounces semisweet chocolate, coarsely chopped
1 14-ounce can (1¼ cups) sweetened condensed milk
½ cup milk
  Dippers such as angel food cake, pound cake, marshmallows, dried apricots, whole strawberries, banana slices, or pineapple chunks

Melt chocolate in a heavy medium saucepan over low heat, stirring constantly. Stir in the sweetened condensed milk and milk; heat through. Transfer to a fondue pot; keep warm over low heat of fondue burner.

powder, or melted chocolate or candy
ating, if desired. Store in a sealed
ntainer in refrigerator. Makes about
40 pieces.

Nutrition facts per piece: 83 cal., 5 g total fat
(2 g sat. fat), 2 mg chol., 6 mg sodium, 10 g carbo.,
0 g fiber, 1 g pro. Daily values: 0% vit. A, 0% vit. C,
0% calcium, 1% iron

Fudge-Filled Thumbprints

*Get the children involved with these
cookie preparations. Let them make
the thumbprint indentations for the
fudge filling.*

- ½ cup butter, softened
- ⅓ cup packed brown sugar
- 1 egg yolk
- ½ teaspoon vanilla
- 1 cup all-purpose flour
- 1 slightly beaten egg white
- ¾ to 1 cup finely chopped pecans
- 4 ounces semisweet chocolate
- 2 tablespoons butter
- 2 teaspoons seedless raspberry
  jam
- ½ cup sifted powdered sugar
- 2 to 3 teaspoons milk
- ¼ teaspoon vanilla

Beat the ½ cup butter in a large
mixing bowl with an electric mixer on
medium to high speed for 30 seconds.
Add brown sugar and beat until
combined. Beat in egg yolk and vanilla
until combined. Beat in as much of the
flour as you can with mixer. Stir in any
remaining flour with a wooden spoon.
Shape dough into 1-inch balls. Roll
balls in egg white and then roll in
pecans. Place 1-inch apart on a lightly
greased cookie sheet. Press your thumb
into the center of each ball.
Bake in a 375° oven for 9 to
11 minutes or until edges are lightly

browned. Transfer to a wire rack and let
cool completely.
For filling, melt chocolate and
2 tablespoons butter in a small
saucepan over low heat, stirring
frequently. Remove from heat. Stir in
raspberry jam until smooth. Let filling
cool slightly. Spoon filling into the
depressions in the cookies. Let stand
until set. (Filled cookies may need to be
refrigerated for 15 to 20 minutes to set
the chocolate.)
For icing, combine the powdered
sugar, 1 teaspoon milk, and ¼ teaspoon
vanilla in a small mixing bowl. Stir in
additional milk, 1 teaspoon at a time,
until of drizzling consistency. Drizzle
over cookies. If planning to store
cookies, do not fill or add icing until just
before serving. Makes about 24 cookies.

Nutrition facts per cookie: 127 cal., 9 g total fat
(4 g sat. fat), 22 mg chol., 52 mg sodium,
12 g carbo., 1 g fiber, 1 g pro. Daily values:
5% vit. A, 0% vit. C, 0% calcium, 3% iron

Double-Chocolate Mocha Biscotti

*Espresso adds to the flavor of these
crunchy Italian confections, which are
dipped in white chocolate.*

- 1 12-ounce package (2 cups)
  miniature semisweet
  chocolate pieces
- ⅓ cup butter, softened
- ⅔ cup sugar
- 2 teaspoons baking powder
- 2 teaspoons instant espresso or
  coffee powder
- 2 eggs
- 1 teaspoon vanilla
- 2 cups all-purpose flour
- 1 cup (6 ounces) white
  baking pieces
- 1 teaspoon shortening

Set aside ½ cup of the miniature
semisweet pieces. Melt remaining
pieces in a small saucepan over low
heat, stirring occasionally.
Meanwhile, beat butter in a large
mixing bowl with an electric mixer on
medium to high speed for 30 seconds.
Add sugar, baking powder, and espresso
or coffee powder; beat until combined.
Beat in melted chocolate, eggs, and
vanilla until combined. Beat in as much
flour as you can with the mixer. Stir in
any remaining flour with a wooden
spoon. Stir in reserved chocolate pieces.
Divide dough in half.
Using lightly floured hands, shape
each portion into an 8-inch-long loaf.
Place rolls about 5 inches apart on a
lightly greased cookie sheet. Flatten to
2½ inches in width.
Bake in a 375° oven for 25 to
30 minutes or until firm and a wooden
toothpick inserted in center comes out
clean. Cool on cookie sheet for 1 hour.
Transfer to a cutting board. Cut
each loaf diagonally into ½-inch-thick
slices. Lay slices, cut sides down, on
the cookie sheet. Bake in a 375° oven
for 10 minutes. Turn slices over and
bake for 10 to 15 minutes more or until
dry and crisp. Remove from cookie
sheet and cool on a wire rack.
Melt white baking pieces and
shortening in a small heavy saucepan
over low heat, stirring occasionally. Dip
one corner of each cookie into melted
mixture. Makes about 30 cookies.

Nutrition facts per cookie: 155 cal., 8 g total fat
(3 g sat. fat), 22 mg chol., 56 mg sodium,
21 g carbo., 0 g fiber, 2 g pro. Daily values:
2% vit. A, 0% vit. C, 2% calcium, 4% iron

111

powder, and soda; beat until combined. Beat in egg and vanilla until combined. Gradually beat in flour mixture.

Shape dough into 1-inch balls; place on ungreased cookie sheet. Press down center of each ball with thumb. Drain maraschino cherries, reserving juice. Place a cherry in the center of each cookie. In a small saucepan combine the chocolate pieces and sweetened condensed milk; heat until chocolate is melted. Stir in 4 teaspoons of the reserved cherry juice.

Spoon about 1 teaspoon of the frosting over each cherry, spreading to cover cherry. (Frosting may be thinned with additional cherry juice, if needed.)

Bake in a 350° oven about 10 minutes or until done. Remove to wire rack; cool. Makes 48 cookies.

Nutrition facts per cookie: 81 cal., 3 g total fat (1 g sat. fat), 11 mg chol., 45 mg sodium, 12 g carbo., 0 g fiber, 1 g pro. Daily values: 2% vit. A, 0% vit. C, 1% calcium, 2% iron

Chocolate-Covered Cherry Cookies

Chocolate-Covered Cherry Cookies

Be sure to use real chocolate (not imitation) because the not-so-real product won't bake properly.

1½ cups all-purpose flour
½ cup unsweetened cocoa powder
½ cup butter, softened
1 cup sugar
¼ teaspoon salt
¼ teaspoon baking powder
¼ teaspoon baking soda
1 egg
1½ teaspoons vanilla
48 undrained maraschino cherries (about one 10-ounce jar)
1 cup semisweet chocolate pieces
½ cup sweetened condensed milk

Combine flour and cocoa powder in a mixing bowl; set aside. Beat butter in a large mixing bowl with an electric mixer on medium to high speed for 30 seconds. Add sugar, salt, baking

German Chocolate Cheesecake

With its nutty-coconut topping, this dreamy cheesecake will remind you of its old-fashioned namesake.

Coconut-Pecan Topping
1 cup graham cracker crumbs
2 tablespoons sugar
⅓ cup butter, melted
¼ cup flaked coconut
¼ cup chopped pecans
4 ounces semisweet chocolate, chopped
3 8-ounce packages cream cheese, softened

¾ cup sugar
½ cup dairy sour cream
2 teaspoons vanilla
2 tablespoons all-purpose flour
3 eggs
   Pecan halves (optional)

Prepare the Coconut-Pecan Topping; set aside.

For crust, combine graham cracker crumbs, the 2 tablespoons sugar, melted butter, coconut, and pecans in a

mixing bowl. Press mixture into the bottom and ½ inch up sides of a 9-inch springform pan. Bake in a 350° oven for 8 to 10 minutes. Cool slightly.

Melt chocolate in a saucepan over low heat. Remove from heat and set aside to cool.

For filling, beat together the cream cheese, ¾ cup sugar, sour cream, and vanilla in a mixing bowl. Add flour and beat well. Add eggs and cooled chocolate; beat until just combined. Turn filling into the cooled crust.

Bake in a 375° oven for 45 to 50 minutes or until the center appears nearly set when you shake it. Cool for 15 minutes. Loosen sides of cheesecake from the sides of the pan. Cool 30 minutes. Remove sides of pan.

Spread Coconut-Pecan Topping over cheesecake. Cover and refrigerate

3 to 24 hours. If desired, garnish with pecan halves. Makes 12 to 14 servings.

COCONUT-PECAN TOPPING: Melt ½ cup butter in a small saucepan. Stir in ¼ cup packed brown sugar, 2 tablespoons half-and-half or light cream, and 2 tablespoons light-colored corn syrup. Cook and stir over medium heat until bubbly. Stir in 1 cup flaked coconut, ½ cup chopped pecans, and 1 teaspoon vanilla. Remove from heat; cool for 5 minutes. Spread over partially cooled cheesecake.

Nutrition facts per serving: 599 cal., 47 g total fat (27 g sat. fat), 155 mg chol., 365 mg sodium, 40 g carbo., 2 g fiber, 9 g pro. Daily values: 41% vit. A, 0% vit. C, 7% calcium, 14% iron

melting chocolate

Chocolate is heat-sensitive and burns easily, especially when it's melted alone. Containers and stirring utensils must be clean and perfectly dry. Small amounts of water may cause melted chocolate to lose its gloss instead of melting smoothly. Here are two ways to melt chocolate easily:

■ To melt on the rangetop: Place cut-up chocolate or chocolate pieces in a heavy saucepan. Melt the chocolate over low heat, stirring often to prevent scorching. Sometimes 1 teaspoon shortening is added for each ½ cup or 3 ounces of chocolate to help the chocolate set up.

■ To melt in a microwave oven: Place up to 6 ounces of chopped chocolate or chocolate pieces in a microwave-safe bowl or measuring cup. Microwave, uncovered, on 100% power (high) for 1½ to 2 minutes or until soft enough to stir smoothly. Stir after 60 seconds; the chocolate pieces or squares won't seem melted until stirred.

113

German Chocolate Cheesecake

Fudge Packages: Cut homemade or purchased fudge into cubes and wrap with colorful foil wrappers. Tie with ribbon or raffia so that the bundles look like tiny packages. Set one package at each place setting for a table decoration or arrange on a plate for gift giving.

In a Twinkling: Garnishes

◀ Lime Bows: Remove long strips of lime peel with a zester. Cut into shorter pieces and tie into bows. Use to decorate desserts or salads.

▲ Candy Ornaments: Prepar Icing (see page 96). Place a p waxed paper on top of a s graph paper to use as a guid decorating bag with a wri spoon icing into bag. Pipe sn designs onto the paper. Sprin white edible glitter and set asi the ornaments are hardened table decorations or add a ribb hang on t

▲ Colorful Cutouts: Using tiny hors d'oeuvre cutters, cut slices of jellied cranberry sauce or red or green sweet peppers into tiny shapes. Use to decorate salads or main dishes.

▲ Chilly and Easy Dessert: Make small scoops of various colors and flavors of ice cream and/or sherbet and stack in a footed dessert dish. Drizzle lightly with chocolate sauce or ice cream topping.

◀ Chocolate Edge: Dip the rim of a dessert dish or glass into melted semisweet chocolate or melted white baking bar. Then dip the rim in a bowl of chopped nuts. Place in the refrigerator for about 20 minutes to set the chocolate. Fill the dish with fruit, ice cream, or sherbet.

▲ Sugared Fruit: Using a clean brush, apply a mixture of water and meringue powder all over a small fresh pear or miniature bunch of grapes. Immediately sprinkle with granulated sugar to give a frosted look to the fruit. Use as a table decoration or to garnish a meat platter, dessert, or fruit and cheese tray.

▶
Whipped Cream Swirl: Instead of topping dessert with a whipped cream dollop, spoon a couple of tablespoons of whipped cream on the empty dessert plate. Using a decorating comb, swirl the cream into an interesting pattern. Add a serving of dessert on top of the cream.

Holiday Fruit Strudel

Every country that celebrates Christmas has special foods associated with the holiday—English fruitcake, Swiss pinecone cake, and German strudel, to name a few. Enjoy your tasty heritage or adopt a new tradition with these favorites.

holiday baking *classics*

Holiday Fruit Strudel

✳

Strudel is a German classic that's popular in much of central Europe. The pastry, made of many layers of a very thin dough, turns crisp and golden brown when baked. We've shortened the pastry preparations by substituting phyllo dough. And, although apples are the most common fruit used for the filling, this recipe includes dried pears, cranberries, and currants for color and flavor.

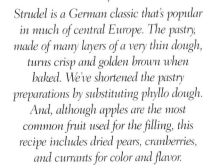

1 large firm pear or tart apple, peeled, cored, and chopped
⅓ cup chopped pecans or walnuts
¼ cup chopped dried pear
¼ cup dried cranberries
3 tablespoons sugar
2 tablespoons dried currants
2 tablespoons finely chopped crystallized ginger
½ teaspoon finely shredded orange peel
¼ cup sugar
¼ teaspoon ground cinnamon
8 sheets frozen phyllo dough, thawed
⅓ cup butter, melted
Eggnog Whipped Cream (optional)
Ground nutmeg (optional)
Orange peel curls (optional)

Stir together fresh pear or apple, pecans or walnuts, dried pear, cranberries, the 3 tablespoons sugar, currants, ginger, and orange peel in a medium mixing bowl; set aside.

Combine the ¼ cup sugar and cinnamon in a small bowl. Reserve 1 teaspoon cinnamon-sugar for top. Lightly brush 1 sheet of phyllo with some of the melted butter (keep remaining phyllo covered). Sprinkle phyllo sheet with some of the cinnamon-sugar mixture. Repeat with remaining sheets of phyllo, butter, and cinnamon-sugar. If necessary, cut off some of the phyllo to make a rectangle about 15×13 inches.

Place fruit filling in a 3- to 4-inch-wide lengthwise strip 2 inches from the closest long edge and 1 inch from the ends. From the closest edge, fold the phyllo over the filling. Roll up the dough and filling.

Place a greased 15×10×1-inch baking pan next to the strudel and place the strudel, seam side down, in the pan. Tuck the ends under. Brush the top lightly with butter and sprinkle with the reserved cinnamon-sugar mixture.

Bake in a 350° oven for 35 minutes or until golden brown. Cool in the baking pan set on a wire rack. Cut into slices with a serrated knife. Serve warm with Eggnog Whipped Cream and garnish with a sprinkling of ground nutmeg and orange peel curls, if desired. Makes 8 servings.

EGGNOG WHIPPED CREAM: Beat ½ cup whipping cream with 1 tablespoon sifted powdered sugar, 2 teaspoons dark rum, ½ teaspoon vanilla, and a dash ground nutmeg until soft peaks form.

Nutrition facts per serving: 247 cal., 12 g total fat (5 g sat. fat), 20 mg chol., 172 mg sodium, 35 g carbo., 2 g fiber, 2 g pro. Daily values: 7% vit. A, 3% vit. C, 1% calcium, 9% iron

Steamed Cranberry Pudding

Remove pudding from Dutch oven and let stand 2 to 3 minutes. Remove foil; unmold onto serving dish. Sprinkle with powdered sugar and garnish with sugared cranberries and fresh mint leaves, if desired. Serve with Hard Sauce. Makes 12 servings.

HARD SAUCE: Beat together 1 cup sifted powdered sugar and ¼ cup softened butter or margarine in a small mixing bowl with an electric mixer on medium speed for 3 to 5 minutes or until well combined. Beat in ½ teaspoon vanilla. Spoon into a serving bowl. Chill sauce to harden. Makes ⅔ cup sauce.

Nutrition facts per serving: 233 cal., 7 g total fat (4 g sat. fat), 35 mg chol., 181 mg sodium, 40 g carbo., 1 g fiber, 3 g pro. Daily values: 7% vit. A, 4% vit. C, 3% calcium, 8% iron

118

Steamed Cranberry Pudding

Cranberries add a distinctly American twist to the original English Plum Pudding.

 2 cups cranberries
 2 cups plus 2 tablespoons all-purpose flour
 ½ cup packed brown sugar
 ⅓ cup granulated sugar
 1 teaspoon baking soda
 1 teaspoon ground cinnamon
 ½ teaspoon ground nutmeg
 ¼ teaspoon ground allspice
 1 cup milk
 1 egg
 2 tablespoons butter or margarine, melted
 Powdered sugar (optional)
 Sugared cranberries (optional) (see Sugared Fruit directions, page 115)
 Fresh mint (optional)
 Hard Sauce

Toss together the 2 cups cranberries and 2 tablespoons flour in a small bowl; set aside.

Stir together the 2 cups flour, brown sugar, granulated sugar, baking soda, cinnamon, nutmeg, and allspice in a large mixing bowl. Add milk, egg, and melted butter; stir until well combined. Stir in cranberry mixture.

Transfer to a well-greased 6-cup metal mold. Cover tightly with foil. Place mold on a rack in a Dutch oven or roasting pan. Add boiling water to just below rack; cover pan.

Bring water to a gentle boil over medium heat. Steam 1 to 1½ hours or until a wooden toothpick inserted in center comes out clean, adding boiling water to Dutch oven occasionally to maintain desired water level.

Zimtstern

Another version of the meringue, these German Christmas delicacies are flavored with cinnamon and shaped like stars.

 2 egg whites
 1½ cups almonds, toasted and ground
 ¾ cup hazelnuts (filberts), toasted and ground
 2 tablespoons all-purpose flour
 1 teaspoon ground cinnamon
 ¼ teaspoon ground nutmeg
 1 cup granulated sugar
 Powdered sugar
 1½ cups sifted powdered sugar
 Milk
 Several drops food coloring

Let egg whites stand in a large mixing bowl at room temperature for 30 minutes. Meanwhile, line 2 large cookie sheets with parchment paper. Combine almonds, hazelnuts, flour, cinnamon, and nutmeg in a medium mixing bowl. Set aside.

Beat egg whites with an electric mixer on medium speed until soft peaks form (tips curl). Gradually add granulated sugar, 1 tablespoon at a time, beating on high speed until stiff peaks form (tips stand straight) and sugar is almost dissolved. Fold nut mixture into egg whites. Cover; let stand for 30 minutes.

Sprinkle some powdered sugar lightly over work surface. Roll dough on surface to ¼-inch thickness. Using a floured 2- to 2½-inch star-shaped cutter, cut dough into stars. Place 1 inch apart on prepared cookie sheets.

Bake in a 325° oven about 10 minutes or until cookies are lightly browned and crisp. Remove cookies and cool completely on wire racks.

For frosting, stir together the 1½ cups powdered sugar and enough milk (1 to 2 tablespoons) to make a thin spreading consistency. Tint frosting with food coloring. Spread on cookies. Makes about 32 cookies.

Nutrition facts per cookie: 99 cal., 5 g total fat (0 g sat. fat), 0 mg chol., 5 mg sodium, 13 g carbo., 1 g fiber, 2 g pro. Daily values: 0% vit. A, 0% vit. C, 1% calcium, 2% iron

Christmas Ice Box Cookies

Housewives of the 1930s, who had just acquired electric refrigeration, considered ice box cookies an improvement over rolled cookies. Ice box cookies do not require rolling but are as thin and crisp as any rolled cookie. This recipe is leavened with baking ammonia, a typical leavening agent used for baking in Denmark around 1900.

  2 cups butter, softened
  3 cups sugar
  ½ teaspoon baking ammonia* or cream of tartar

     Dash salt
  1 egg
  4½ to 5 cups all-purpose flour
     Coarse blue-colored sugar and/or pearl sugar (optional)

Beat butter in a large mixing bowl with an electric mixer on medium to high speed for 30 seconds. Add sugar, baking ammonia or cream of tartar, and salt; beat until combined. Beat in egg until combined. Beat in as much of the flour as you can with the mixer. Stir in enough remaining flour to make a stiff dough, using a wooden spoon. Divide dough into thirds. Shape dough into logs about 1½ inches in diameter and 9 inches long. Wrap the logs and chill for 1 to 3 hours or until firm.

Cut rolls into ¼-inch-thick slices. Place slices 1 inch apart on ungreased cookie sheet. Sprinkle with blue and/or pearl decorating sugar, if desired.

Bake in a 375° oven for 8 to 10 minutes or until bottoms and edges of cookies are golden brown. Makes about 90 cookies.

*Note: Baking ammonia is available at most pharmacies. If you use baking ammonia, use caution when opening the container and when opening the oven door after baking the cookies; irritating ammonia-like fumes may be produced. (Cream of tartar is an acceptable substitute, although cookies made with it are less crisp than those made with baking ammonia.)

Nutrition facts per cookie: 83 cal., 4 g total fat (3 g sat. fat), 13 mg chol., 42 mg sodium, 11 g carbo., 0 g fiber, 1 g pro. Daily values: 3% vit. A, 0% vit. C, 0% calcium, 1% iron

119

Christmas Ice Box Cookies

Zimtstern

Dark Fruitcake

English Tea Ring

Dark Fruitcake

Fruitcake, which originated in England, is traditionally served there at christenings and weddings, usually coated in marzipan and royal icing. Here it is considered a Christmas specialty and comes in many variations from light to dark, very cakey to densely fruited.

    1½ cups all-purpose flour
     1 teaspoon ground cinnamon
     ½ teaspoon baking powder
     ¼ teaspoon baking soda
     ¼ teaspoon ground nutmeg
     ¼ teaspoon ground allspice
     ¼ teaspoon ground cloves
     2 eggs
     ¼ cup packed brown sugar
     ¼ cup apple jelly, melted
     ⅓ cup apple or orange juice
     ⅓ cup butter, melted
     2 tablespoons mild-flavored
        molasses
     ¾ cup diced mixed candied fruits
        and peels
     ⅓ cup snipped pitted dates
     ⅓ cup snipped dried figs
     ⅓ cup raisins
     ⅓ cup golden raisins
        Fruit juice or brandy

Grease an 8×4×2-inch loaf pan. Line bottom and sides of pan with brown paper; grease paper.

Combine flour, cinnamon, baking powder, baking soda, nutmeg, allspice, and cloves in a large mixing bowl. Beat eggs in a medium bowl. Add sugar, apple jelly, juice, butter, and molasses; stir until combined. Stir egg mixture into flour mixture. Stir in candied fruits, dates, figs, and raisins just until combined. Pour into prepared pan.

Bake in a 300° oven for 1¼ to 1½ hours or until a wooden toothpick inserted near the center comes out clean. (Cover pan loosely with foil after 1 hour of baking to prevent overbrowning.) Cool in pan on wire rack. Remove from pan.

English Tea Ring

Teatime is taken very seriously in England, and there are always goodies, such as this yeasty fruit and nut roll. Sometimes this tasty sweet bread is referred to as a Swedish tea ring.

120

     3 to 3¼ cups all-purpose flour
     1 package active dry yeast
     ¾ cup milk
     ¼ cup butter or margarine
     ¼ cup sugar
     ½ teaspoon salt
     1 beaten egg
     ½ teaspoon vanilla
     2 tablespoons butter or
        margarine, melted
     ¼ cup sugar
     ¾ cup chopped walnuts, pecans,
        or almonds
     ¾ cup diced mixed candied fruits
        and peels or golden raisins
     1 beaten egg yolk
     1 tablespoon water
        Powdered sugar

Combine 1 cup of the flour and the yeast in a large mixing bowl. Heat milk, the ¼ cup butter, ¼ cup sugar, and salt in a small saucepan until warm (120° to 130°). Add to flour mixture along with egg and vanilla. Beat with an electric mixer on medium speed for 30 seconds, scraping bowl constantly. Beat on high speed for 3 minutes, scraping bowl occasionally. Stir in as much remaining flour as you can.

Turn out on a lightly floured surface. Knead in enough of the remaining flour to make a moderately soft dough that is smooth and elastic (3 to 5 minutes total). Shape into a ball. Place dough in a greased bowl; turn once to grease surface of the dough. Cover and let rise in a warm place until double (about 1½ hours).

Punch dough down. Turn out onto a lightly floured surface. Roll into a 16×10-inch rectangle. Brush with the 2 tablespoons melted butter. Combine ¼ cup sugar, the nuts, and candied fruits and peels or raisins. Sprinkle nut mixture evenly over rectangle. Roll up jelly-roll style from the long side and seal the edge.

Shape roll into a ring on a greased baking sheet. Using scissors, snip almost to the center at 1-inch intervals. Pull sections apart and twist slightly. Cover and let rise until nearly double (45 to 60 minutes). Combine egg yolk and water; brush over ring.

Bake in a 375° oven for 25 minutes or until done. Remove from baking sheet; cool on a wire rack. Dust with powdered sugar. Makes 16 servings.

Nutrition facts per serving: 220 cal., 9 g total fat (3 g sat. fat), 39 mg chol., 128 mg sodium, 31 g carbo., 1 g fiber, 4 g pro. Daily values: 8% vit. A, 0% vit. C, 2% calcium, 8% iron

Wrap fruitcake in 100% cotton cheesecloth moistened with fruit juice or brandy. Overwrap with foil. Store in the refrigerator for 2 to 8 weeks to mellow flavors of the fruitcake. Remoisten cheesecloth once a week or as needed. Makes 16 servings.

Nutrition facts per serving: 181 cal., 5 g total fat (3 g sat. fat), 37 mg chol., 87 mg sodium, 34 g carbo., 1 g fiber, 2 g pro. Daily values: 5% vit. A, 0% vit. C, 3% calcium, 7% iron

Pinecone Cake

✳

Tannzapfen, another name for this cake, is a Swiss Christmas specialty. Shaped like a pinecone, a basic sponge cake is spread with buttercream, then decorated with toasted almonds.

1½   cups all-purpose flour
1½   teaspoons baking powder
¼   teaspoon salt
3   eggs
1½   cups granulated sugar
¾   cup milk
3   tablespoons butter
1   teaspoon vanilla
    Sifted powdered sugar
    Buttercream Frosting
2   cups sliced almonds, toasted*

For cake, combine flour, baking powder, and salt in a small bowl. Beat eggs in a large mixing bowl with an electric mixer on high speed about 4 minutes or until thick. Gradually add the 1½ cups sugar; beat on medium speed about 4 minutes or until sugar dissolves, scraping bottom and sides of bowl occasionally. Add flour mixture to egg mixture; stir just until combined.

Heat and stir milk and butter in a small saucepan until butter melts. Stir into batter. Stir in vanilla and mix well. Pour the batter into a greased and floured 15×10×1-inch baking pan; spread batter evenly.

Bake in a 350° oven for 20 to 25 minutes or until a wooden toothpick comes out clean. Cool in pan 10 minutes. Loosen edges of cake from pan and turn cake out onto a towel sprinkled with powdered sugar. Remove pan and let cake cool completely. Prepare Buttercream Frosting.

Make 2 pinecone shape patterns (egg shapes) on a piece of paper—one 10 inches long and 6 inches wide and one 9 inches long and 4½ inches wide. Trace and cut one 10-inch and two 9-inch shapes from the cake. Reserve cake scraps. Place one 9-inch shape on a serving plate. Spread with Buttercream Frosting. Top with 10-inch shape; spread with buttercream. Top with remaining 9-inch shape and spread with buttercream. Cut and arrange scraps on flat cake top (as shown), giving a rounded top to the pinecone (about 5 to 6 inches long and 3 to 4 inches wide). Any remaining cake scraps may be saved for another use. Frost entire cake with remaining buttercream, filling in uneven edges to make a smooth rounded shape.

Starting at the point of the pinecone, place almond slices into the buttercream, pointed side up and slightly overlapping (as shown), until cake is completely covered to resemble a pinecone. Chill 1 hour. (Cake can be covered and chilled up to 1 day before serving. Let stand at room temperature about 30 minutes before serving.) Dust lightly with additional sifted powdered sugar to resemble snow. Slice to serve. Makes 12 servings.

*Note: You may need to purchase and toast extra nuts to allow for broken nut pieces. Save any remaining or broken toasted almonds for another use.

BUTTERCREAM FROSTING: Combine 1 cup granulated sugar and 2 tablespoons unsweetened cocoa powder in a small heavy saucepan; stir until combined. Stir in ⅓ cup water and 1 tablespoon instant coffee crystals. Bring to boiling. Remove from heat. Gradually stir about *half* of the sugar mixture into 6 slightly beaten egg yolks. Return all of the egg yolk mixture to saucepan. Bring to a gentle boil; reduce heat. Cook and stir for 2 minutes. Remove from heat. Stir in 1 teaspoon vanilla. Cool to room temperature. Beat 1½ cups softened unsalted butter in a large mixing bowl with an electric mixer on high speed until fluffy. Add cooled sugar mixture, beating until combined. If necessary, chill the frosting until it is of spreading consistency.

Nutrition facts per serving: 637 cal., 42 g total fat (19 g sat. fat), 231 mg chol., 153 mg sodium, 61 g carbo., 3 g fiber, 10 g pro. Daily values: 43% vit. A, 0% vit. C, 13% calcium, 14% iron

121

's how...

1

Arrange large broken cake scraps for top layer of Pinecone Cake, giving the top of the cake a rounded appearance, like an egg.

2

Starting at the tip of the frosted cake, insert nuts in rows, pointed side up and overlapping slightly as shown, giving a pinecone look to the cake.

GIVING

Stumped for a good gift idea?

Coming up with the perfect gift is like solving an equation: recipient's interests+your talents=great gift. For example, everyone likes to eat, right? If you love to cook, a gift from the kitchen is a great way to share your talents. See pages 138–43 for some mouthwatering treats. If your culinary skills aren't so hot but you're handy with crafts, buy prepared gourmet foods and put your talents into the presentation. Stitch up a wine cozy (inspired by tea cozies) to go with a bottle of your favorite vintage or pile bakery cookies on a plate you've etched with a festive design. For gardening friends, pot up amaryllis bulbs or tree seedlings. Check out the crafts for kids on pages 152–53, too—they're just as much fun for adults. Whenever you put your time and talents into a gift, you enrich its value, because the best gift you can give is yourself.

from the HEART

Present your host or hostess with one of these handmade gifts, and your creativity and thoughtfulness will be remembered long after the holidays are over.

thoughtful tokens

Turn pinecones into topiaries to display singly or in a group. These are small enough that your hostess can easily find a spot for one. They're also great to have on hand when you need a gift in a hurry.

Although etiquette books advise against showing up at a party with cut flowers—it's inconvenient for the hostess to stop and find a vase for them—it's okay to send them afterward to express your thanks. To give the

flowers a personal touch, deliver them yourself in a thrift-shop vase you've painted with Christmas designs. Edible or drinkable gifts are good, too. For a more memorable presentation, offer baked goods on a plate you've etched yourself, or wrap up wine or sherry in a "cozy" or wine scarf.

Painted Vase

here's how...

1 Referring to the photograph *at left*, paint rows of lines, squiggles, dots, spirals, and squares onto the vase. Follow any embossed lines as a guide in creating a repeating pattern. Don't worry about making the lines uniform: if they're thick and thin, it adds to the whimsical charm of the design. If you want a more controlled pattern, draw your design on tissue paper and tape it to the inside of the vase. Paint over the designs, then move the pattern to the next area and repeat.

2 To heat-set the paint and make it permanent and waterproof, bake the finished vase in the oven, following the manufacturer's instructions.

Mini-Topiaries

here's how...

1 Following the manufacturer's instructions, use adhesive size to paint designs on the terra-cotta pots. When the adhesive is tacky to the touch, apply the metal leaf. Spritz the pinecones with bright-gold spray paint.

2 Place gravel or small rocks in the bottom of the pot to balance the weight of the pinecone. Push the plastic foam ball into the pot so it fits snugly.

3 To make a topiary with a trunk, cut a twig to the desired length and sharpen one end to a point with a knife. Use hot glue to attach the pinecone to the blunt end. Push the pointed end into the plastic foam ball.

4 To make a trunkless topiary, glue the pinecone directly to the plastic foam.

5 Cover the plastic foam ball with sheet moss or sphagnum moss. For the tall topiary, spray a few tiny pinecones gold and glue them around the base.

SHOPPING LIST:

clear glass vase
    (ours is from a
    secondhand shop)
From a crafts store:
    Delta CeramDecor
    paints: red, green,
    and white
    paintbrush

124

SHOPPING LIST

From a hardware store:
  assorted small terra-cotta
    pots with saucers
  gravel or small rocks
From a crafts store:
  composition metal leaf
    and adhesive size or a
    gilding kit
  plastic foam ball
  bright-gold spray paint
  sheet moss or sphagnum
    moss
  hot-glue gun and
    glue sticks
From your yard:
  assorted large and
    small pinecones
  ¼-inch-diameter twigs

Wine Bottle Cozies

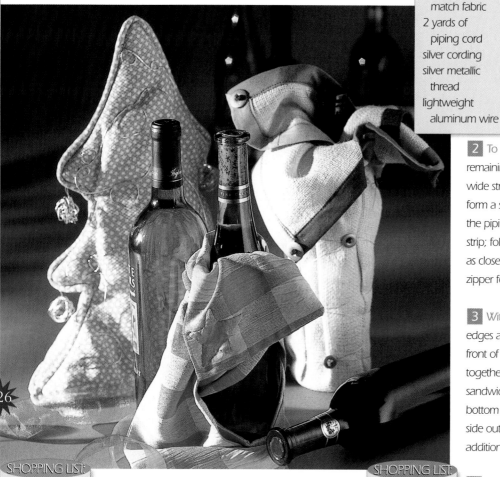

Christmas Tree

here's how...

1 Enlarge the pattern below. Cut two tree shapes each from the fabric and batting. Baste the batting to the wrong side of the fabric.

2 To cover your own piping, cut the remaining fabric on the bias into 2½-inch-wide strips. Stitch the strips together to form a straight 55-inch-long strip. Center the piping cord on the wrong side of the strip; fold the strip over the cord and stitch as close to the cord as possible, using the zipper foot on your sewing machine.

3 With right sides facing and raw edges aligned, stitch the piping to the front of the tree. Stitch the two tree shapes together, right sides facing and piping sandwiched in between. Leave the bottom edge open. Turn the tree right side out and stuff the points with additional batting to fill out the shape.

4 Turn under the bottom edge of the tree back and topstitch the hem in place.

5 Arrange silver cording on the tree front as desired and tack it in place with the silver metallic thread.

Napkin Drape

here's how...

1 Place the wine bottle in the center of the napkin. Bring the napkin up around the bottle and wrap it with aluminum wire to hold it in place. Wrap wire several times along the length of the bottle, crisscrossing the wire.

2 Where the wires cross, hand-sew a button, then sew a bead on top.

3 Sew a button, topped by a bead, to each corner of the napkin.

Wine Scarf

here's how...

1 From the rayon fabric, cut two 6½x23-inch strips.

2 From the tracing paper, cut a small freehand star. Using the paper as a pattern, cut the star from the 3-inch square of coordinating fabric, adding ½ inch all around. Turn under the ½-inch allowance and press. Blind-stitch the star to the right side of one strip of rayon in one corner.

3 Pin the two rayon strips together, right sides facing. Stitch, leaving a small opening for turning. Turn and press; whip-stitch the opening closed.

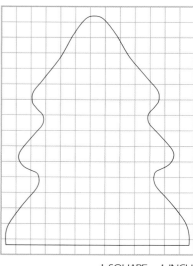

1 SQUARE = 1 INCH

126

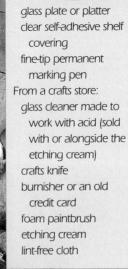

SHOPPING LIST

glass plate or platter
clear self-adhesive shelf
covering
fine-tip permanent
marking pen
From a crafts store:
glass cleaner made to
work with acid (sold
with or alongside the
etching cream)
crafts knife
burnisher or an old
credit card
foam paintbrush
etching cream
lint-free cloth

Etching Precautions:

1 Make sure the room's temperature is above 70 degrees.

2 Provide good ventilation.

3 Cover the work area with newspaper.

4 Work near a source of running water.

5 Wear a long-sleeve garment and rubber gloves to protect your skin from the etching cream. To be on the safe side, protect your eyes from possible splashes by wearing glasses or goggles.

Etched-Glass Plates

Etch a clear or colored glass plate with the words of a Christmas carol or other holiday greeting, then mound cookies or candy on the plate to leave with your hostess.

here's how...

1 Clean the glass plate with the special glass cleaner. (It is important to use the special glass cleaner because it won't leave a film.)

2 Create words on a computer, and use the printout for your pattern. Tape the pattern to the back of the plate.

Cover the plate with clear self-adhesive shelf paper, piecing strips as needed to cover the surface completely. Trace the words with the permanent marking pen, then remove the pattern from the back of the plate.

Cut out the letters using the crafts knife. Press the edges of the letters firmly, using the burnisher or an old credit card to seal the edges. (Don't use your fingers—the oil from your skin may interfere with the action of the etching cream.)

5 To prepare the plate for etching, lightly reclean the exposed glass with the special glass cleaner. Use a damp, not wet, cloth. Pat dry.

Check the list of precautions, above, before you begin working with the etching cream. Using the foam paintbrush, apply a thick layer of etching cream over the stencil cutouts. Gently move the cream around the area to eliminate air bubbles. Wait 5 to 6 minutes, then rinse off the etching cream.

7 Remove the contact paper to expose the etching.

Make the gift wrap a gift in itself. Match the fabric to the package contents to give a tantalizing hint of what's inside.

two gifts in one

Cotton holiday tea towels are perfect for presenting baked goods such as bread or pans of cookies or gingerbread. And what else should a well-dressed gift of jewelry or clothing wear but a coordinating silk scarf?

Tea Towel Wraps

here's how...

Bread Wrap

1 Place the towel right side down on a flat surface.

2 Fold in the towel's long edges until the width equals the length of the loaf plus about ½ inch. Position the loaf crosswise in the center of the towel.

3 Bring the short, unfolded edges together over the top of the bread. Holding the two edges together as one, fold them down a couple of times to make a snug wrapping around the bread.

4 Wrap the ribbon around the center of the loaf and tie it into a bow. Trim with a sprig of fresh Christmas greenery and artificial berries.

SHOPPING LIST:

FOR LOAF OF BREAD
- tea towel (about 17x25 inches)
- baked loaf of bread
- 1 yard of 1-inch-wide sheer ribbon
- sprigs of fresh greenery and artificial berries

SHOPPING LIST:

FOR PAN OF COOKIES OR GINGERBREAD
- tea towel (about 18x26½ inches)
- gingerbread or baked goods in a 9x9-inch aluminum pan
- plastic wrap
- twist ties
- 1⅓ yards of ⅛-inch-wide red double-face satin ribbon

Pan Wrap

1 Place the towel right side down on a flat surface.

2 Cover the pan with plastic wrap, if necessary, to preserve the freshness of your baked goods. Center the pan on one half of the towel. Bring the other half of the towel over the top of the pan so the short end extends beyond the pan's edge by about 1 inch. Adjust the position of the pan, if necessary, to center the holiday motif on the top. Open the towel out.

3 Fold the bottom short end of the towel over the pan of cookies.

4 Fold the long sides of the towel over the sides of the pan, then fold the top of the towel over the pan.

5 Pinch the towel at each corner around the top of the pan, temporarily holding it in place with twist ties.

6 Cut the ribbon into quarters. Tie a ribbon around each corner, and remove the twist ties.

128

Scarf Wrap

here's how...

1 Place the scarf right side down on a flat surface.

2 Place the gift box in the center with its corners pointing toward the scarf's sides.

3 Gather the corners of the scarf together at the center top of the box and temporarily secure with a twist tie. Tie the

ribbon around the gathers, and remove the twist tie.

4 Slip one Chinese coin onto each corner of the scarf and knot the scarf to hold the coin in place.

*Note: Check bead stores, coin dealers, or stamp and coin shops for Chinese coins; they're also available at some import shops. For a similar effect, use copper or gold washers from a hardware store, or use large pony beads from a crafts store.

129

Silk Bow

here's how...

1 To give the tissue paper texture, crumple it and then smooth it out before wrapping it around the gift box (save the excess tissue paper for stuffing the loops of the bow later).

2 Wrap the scarf around the length of the gift box and temporarily hold it in place at the top with the rubber band. Set the box aside.

3 Knot the ends of the gold elastic cord. Fold the cord in half, creating a doubled strand. Wrap the doubled strand around the rubber band, slipping the knotted ends through the loop of the cord. Pull tight.

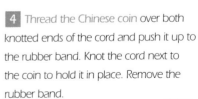

4 Thread the Chinese coin over both knotted ends of the cord and push it up to the rubber band. Knot the cord next to the coin to hold it in place. Remove the rubber band.

5 Tie the scarf into a bow. To give the loops more body, lightly stuff them with scraps of the gold tissue paper.

Recycle holiday greeting cards to make these petite gift boxes. They're perfect for holding jewelry or other small items—a rich piece of candy, a poem, or a personal message.

little *boxes*

For Christmas, you can hang these boxes on the tree as little surprises to hand out on Christmas morning. For Hanukkah or Kwanzaa, use heavy paper or greeting cards to make the boxes and put one at each place setting for the family meal.

"Tube" Pillow Packet

here's how...

1 Cut away the back of the card, except for a 1-inch-wide flap next to the fold. This is the gluing flap.

Working on the wrong side of the card, mark the center of the front panel at the top and bottom edges. Fold the sides to the center marks (the glue flap should be folded).

3 Open out the glue flap. Glue the flap to the inside of the card, creating a flat tube.

4 Mark down ⅝ inch from the center top and up ⅝ inch from the center bottom of the tube. Note: This distance can vary, depending on the size of the card.

On the right side of the tube, draw, then lightly score, an arc at the top and bottom. To draw the arc, use a round cup, glass, or bottle with a

diameter about 1 inch bigger than the width of the flat, folded card. Use the crafts knife or empty ballpoint pen to make the scoring line. Turn the tube over and repeat on the opposite side.

Insert a small gift, then push the scored arcs in to close the top and bottom of the packet.

131

Folded "Purse" Box

here's how...

1 On the wrong side of the card front, draw a square, centering the card's design. At the center of one side, draw a ¾x1⅝-inch rectangle for the tab. Cut out the shape.

2 Make a folding gauge as follows: cut a strip of paper the length of one side of the square and fold it into thirds. Also mark the center of the strip by folding it in half.

3 Using the gauge and a pencil and working on the wrong side of the card, mark thirds on all four sides of the square. Mark the center on two opposite sides (not the tab side—see Diagram 1).

4 With the empty ballpoint pen, score the "thirds" lines, creating a tic-tac-toe grid (Diagram 1). Also, score the grid with diagonal lines. On the side opposite the tab, cut a

⅞-inch slit about ⅜ inch from the edge.

5 Fold the card along the horizontal and vertical lines, then along the diagonal lines (Diagram 2). Fold all edges up, interlocking the diagonal folds.

6 To close the box, gently bend the tab and insert it into the slit (Diagram 3).

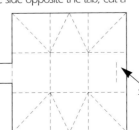

slit

Diagram 1

Diagram 2

Diagram 3

Using a hot-glue gun, glue dried bay leaves from the grocery store in a wreath shape to the top of a package. Add two star anise for the "bow." Dress up a plain brown box with cinnamon sticks and a large or medium-size jingle bell, tied in place with wire-edge organdy ribbon. Make a gift tag from art paper; cut a small slit in the top of the tag and tie short cinnamon sticks to the top of the tag with gold ribbon or cord.

In a Twinkling: Packages

◀ Instead of a bow, top a package with inexpensive glass ball ornaments. (This is a good way to use ornaments that have broken on one side but look fine otherwise.) Use three different sizes and attach them to the package with a hot-glue gun. Add curls of wired star garland for a festive finish.

▲ Put odds and ends to creative use to give packages an elegant look. Use scraps of ribbon and cording to make a bow and glue it to the box. Spray silk ivy leaves silver and glue them over the bow.

▲ Your packages will jingle all the way when you decorate them with bells in assorted sizes. Use a hot-glue gun and glue sticks to attach the jingle bells in a free-form design, and add a knotted ribbon for an accent.

▲ Instead of tying packages with ribbon, use shoelaces! Braid three pairs of neon-colored shoelaces together and wrap the braid around the box. Secure it with a rubber band, then unbraid the ends up to the rubber band and loop the tails through it to make a bow. Or tie metallic shoelaces around a box. Cut a free-form star from heavy paper and punch two holes in the center. Pull the shoelaces through the holes and tie them in a knot.

▶

Use a fancy ponytail holder instead of ribbon to dress up a small package. Tie on a jingle bell or small cluster of artificial fruit with organdy ribbon for a finishing touch.

Blooming bulbs make glorious holiday gifts to enjoy right away. Or for a present that looks to the future, pot evergreen seedlings for your gardening friends.

gifts that *grow*

Blooming Amaryllis

here's how...

Paperwhite narcissus and amaryllis are two classics for forcing into early bloom for the holidays, but you can also try hyacinths, crocuses, certain daffodils, tulips, and irises. Check bulb catalogs or your local nursery for selections recommended for forcing. If your friends have brown thumbs, they'll appreciate a pot of bulbs at the point of blooming—follow the instructions at right to bring amaryllis to the perfect stage for presentation. If your friends are do-it-yourselfers, package the bulbs with a container, potting soil, and instructions so they can enjoy the process themselves.

1 Soak the roots of the amaryllis bulb in a small dish of water for about an hour.

2 Put a few inches of the potting soil in the bottom of the terra-cotta pot and tamp firm.

3 Set the bulb in the center of the pot. Make sure it sits high enough so that the neck of the bulb will protrude just above the rim of the pot.

4 Fill in around the bulb with potting soil, firming the soil with your fingertips. Water thoroughly. Keep the potted bulb in a warm, bright spot, and rotate it often.

SPLITTING BULBS: If another growth appears after your amaryllis has flowered, you can slice or break off the bulblet and its greenery from the main bulb. Be sure to keep a healthy handful of roots attached.

4

tips for other bulbs

■ Tulips, hyacinths, muscari, and crocuses can be forced into early bloom as well. Use a container with drainage holes. Add enough soil so that when you position the bulbs, their tips are about even with the rim of the pot. It's okay to crowd the bulbs, but they shouldn't touch. Fill in around them with soil to within ¼ to ½ inch of the rim. Water the soil, then put the pots in a dark place where temperatures stay between 40 and 50 degrees Fahrenheit. A basement, unheated garage, or refrigerator works well—just be sure the bulbs don't freeze. Check the soil from time to time and water as necessary to keep it damp. Roots will be forming, and you don't want the soil to dry out. Let the bulbs chill for 8 to 16 weeks or until 1 inch of growth appears.. Then move the pots to a brightly lit location where the temperature remains between 50 and 60 degrees Fahrenheit. Water often enough to keep the soil moist. The bulbs should bloom in a month or so.

■ Paperwhite and Soleil d'Or narcissus don't need to be chilled. Plant them in soil or nestle them into a 2- to 3-inch deep layer of pebbles, marbles, or gravel in a watertight container (such as a glazed ceramic dish or a brass box). The bulbs should be one-half to one-third submerged among the pebbles. Keep the water level just below the bottoms of the bulbs.

■ Hyacinths will root in water; look for hyacinth glasses in garden centers and nursery catalogs. Fill the glass to the neck, then position the bulb in the top portion of the glass. Place the glass in a cool, dark spot until the roots reach about 4 inches, then move the glasses to a sunny location.

■ Any bulbs you force in soil can be planted outdoors in spring. Remove the spent flowers and continue watering the potted bulbs until you can plant them outdoors. It may take a couple of years for the bulbs to bloom again, and the flowers may be smaller than they were the first year. Bulbs forced in water will be completely spent after blooming and won't rebloom outdoors.

Reblooming Tips:

1 Pinch off the blossoms as soon as they start to droop and wither so that the plant won't waste energy trying to produce seeds.

2 After flowering, cut flower stalks so that only 2 to 4 inches remain. Place the pot in a warm, sunny spot. Water the stalks whenever the top of the potting soil feels dry. Fertilize once or twice a month with a balanced soluble fertilizer.

3 Put the plant outside in full to nearly full sun when spring warms up.

4 As cold weather approaches, stop watering and feeding to force the plant into dormancy. You can turn the pot over so that the plant doesn't receive any rainfall.

5 Remove the foliage only after it turns yellow and dies.

6 Before the first frost, place the potted bulb in a cool (50 to 60 degrees), dark, dry place, such as a basement.

7 In November, bring the plant upstairs, and resume watering and feeding.

8 There's always a chance that the amaryllis won't rebloom the first year, so be prepared to give it at least one more opportunity.

Little Trees

Give a gift of future Christmas trees with evergreen seedlings. Choose spruce, pine, or fir, according to the species recommended for your area. Check with a local nursery for seedlings. Plant them in potting soil in terra-cotta pots; the ones shown *at right* are Italian rose pots, available from specialty garden centers and garden catalogs. Cover the soil with pads of reindeer moss. This is available from floral-supply shops and crafts stores. If it's dry when you buy it, place the moss in a plastic bag and sprinkle it with water. Seal the bag and let the moss absorb moisture until it's soft again. Tie organdy ribbon around each little tree and attach a card with the name of the species and instructions for its care—for example, "Set the pot in a sunny place and water the soil well once a week. In the spring, plant the seedling outdoors."

137

Chocolate-Peppermint
Biscotti

There's really no better to way to say "happy holidays" than with a homemade gift. Everyone enjoys receiving freshly prepared holiday treats from a loved one's kitchen. Don't forget—a pretty presentation makes any gift all the more special.

gifts *from the* kitchen

Chocolate-Peppermint Biscotti

Wrap several of the biscotti in plastic wrap and insert into a cone-shaped ornament or a coffee cup along with a package of flavored coffee.

⅔ cup butter, softened
1⅓ cups sugar
1 tablespoon baking powder
⅛ teaspoon salt
4 eggs
½ teaspoon peppermint extract
4 cups all-purpose flour
1½ cups semisweet chocolate pieces, melted and cooled (see page 113)
½ cup coarsely crushed striped round peppermint candies or candy canes
2 tablespoons all-purpose flour

Beat butter in a large mixing bowl with an electric mixer on medium to high speed for 30 seconds. Add sugar, baking powder, and salt; beat until combined. Beat in eggs and peppermint extract until combined. Beat in as much of the 4 cups flour as you can with the mixer. Stir in any remaining flour with a wooden spoon.

Divide dough evenly in half; transfer one half to another bowl. Into one half of the dough stir the melted chocolate. Into the other half of the dough stir the crushed candy and the 2 tablespoons flour until combined.

Divide each half of dough into 3 equal portions. With lightly floured hands, shape each portion into a 14-inch-long rope. Place a rope of each color side by side on an ungreased cookie sheet. Twist ropes around each other several times. Flatten slightly to 2 inches in width. On another cookie sheet, repeat with the other ropes, placing twists about 4 inches apart on the cookie sheet.

Bake one cookie sheet at a time in a 375° oven for 20 to 25 minutes or until lightly browned. Cool on cookie sheet for 1 hour or until completely cool.

Transfer to a cutting board. Using a serrated knife, cut each loaf crosswise (or diagonally) into ½-inch-thick slices. Lay slices, cut sides down, on the cookie sheet. Bake in a 325° oven for 10 minutes. Turn slices to the other side and bake 10 to 15 minutes more or until dry and crisp. Remove and cool on wire rack. Makes about 54 cookies.

Nutrition facts per cookie: 105 cal., 4 g total fat (2 g sat. fat), 22 mg chol., 54 mg sodium, 16 g carbo., 0 g fiber, 2 g pro. Daily values: 2% vit. A, 0% vit. C, 2% calcium, 4% iron

Buttery Cashew Brittle

140

Buttery Cashew Brittle

Add a small container of this candy to a cookie tray for a special treat. The recipient will find that cashews are a wonderful replacement for the more expected peanuts. This candy also can be made with peanuts, almonds, or macadamia nuts.

    2 cups sugar
    1 cup light-colored corn syrup
    ½ cup water
    1 cup butter
    3 cups (about 12 ounces)
         raw cashews
    1 teaspoon baking soda, sifted

Combine sugar, corn syrup, and water in a 3-quart saucepan. Cook and stir until sugar dissolves. Bring mixture to boiling; add butter and stir until butter is melted. Clip a candy thermometer to side of pan. Reduce heat to medium-low; continue boiling at a moderate, steady rate, stirring occasionally, until thermometer registers 280°, the soft-crack stage (about 35 minutes).

Stir in cashews; continue cooking over medium-low heat, stirring frequently until thermometer registers 300°, the hard-crack stage (10 to 15 minutes more).

Remove pan from heat; remove thermometer. Quickly stir in the baking soda, mixing thoroughly. Pour mixture onto 2 buttered baking sheets or 2 buttered 15×10×1-inch pans.

As the cashew brittle cools, stretch it out by lifting and pulling with 2 forks from the edges. Loosen from pans as soon as possible; pick up sections and break them into bite-size pieces. Store tightly covered. Makes about 2½ pounds (72 servings).

Nutrition facts per serving: 90 cal., 5 g total fat (2 g sat. fat), 7 mg chol., 47 mg sodium, 11 g carbo., 0 g fiber, 1 g pro. Daily values: 2% vit. A, 0% vit. C, 0% calcium, 3% iron

Cracker Snack Mix

Pack the mix in a decorative tin or tightly covered bowl that also can be used as a serving container.

    ½ cup butter or margarine
    1 tablespoon Worcestershire
         sauce
    1 teaspoon chili powder
    ¼ teaspoon bottled hot
         pepper sauce
    5 cups oyster crackers
    3 cups corn chips
    3 cups pretzel sticks
    2 cups shelled raw pumpkin
         seeds (pepitas)
    ⅓ cup grated Parmesan cheese

Cook and stir butter, Worcestershire sauce, chili powder, and hot pepper sauce in a medium saucepan over medium-low until butter melts. Combine crackers, corn chips, pretzel sticks, and pumpkin seeds in a large roasting pan. Drizzle butter mixture over cracker mixture; toss to coat.

Bake in a 300° oven for 30 minutes, stirring once. Sprinkle with Parmesan cheese; toss to mix. Spread on foil and cool. Store in an airtight container. Makes 24 (½-cup) servings.

Nutrition facts per serving: 179 cal., 12 g total fat (2 g sat. fat), 6 mg chol., 273 mg sodium, 15 g carbo., 1 g fiber, 5 g pro. Daily values: 4% vit. A, 2% vit. C, 2% calcium, 10% iron

Cranberry Brioche

Include freshly baked brioche with packets of dried cranberries or cherries, assorted preserves, and brioche pans in a basket lined with a holiday kitchen towel or napkin.

    1 package active dry yeast
    ¼ cup warm water (105° to 115°)
    ½ cup butter or margarine,
         softened

⅓ cup sugar
1 teaspoon salt
4 cups all-purpose flour
½ cup milk
4 eggs
½ cup dried cranberries or tart red cherries
¼ cup chopped candied citron (optional)
¼ cup dried currants or snipped raisins
1 tablespoon sugar

Dissolve yeast in warm water in a small bowl. Beat butter, the ⅓ cup sugar, and salt in a large mixing bowl with an electric mixer on medium to high speed until fluffy. Add 1 cup of the flour and the milk to beaten mixture. Separate 1 of the eggs. Add the egg yolk and 3 whole eggs to flour mixture. (Chill remaining egg white.) Add dissolved yeast to flour mixture; beat well. Stir in cranberries or cherries, citron, and currants or raisins. Stir in remaining flour with a wooden spoon.

Place dough in a greased bowl. Cover and let rise in a warm place until double (about 2 hours). Refrigerate for 6 to 24 hours.

Grease 24 individual brioche pans or 2½-inch muffin pans; set aside. Stir down dough. Turn out onto a floured surface. Divide into 4 equal portions. Set 1 portion aside. Divide remaining 3 portions into 8 pieces each. Shape each piece into a ball, pulling edges under to make a smooth top. Place a ball in each prepared brioche pan or muffin cup. Divide remaining dough into 24 pieces; shape into small balls. Make a deep indentation in middle of each large ball with your thumb. Press a small ball into each indentation.

Combine reserved egg white and the 1 tablespoon sugar in a small bowl. Brush mixture over rolls. Cover and let rise in a warm place until nearly double (about 45 to 60 minutes).

Bake in a 375° oven for 13 to 15 minutes or until tops are golden. Remove from pans or muffin cups; cool on wire racks. Makes 24 brioche.

Nutrition facts per brioche: 144 cal., 5 g total fat (3 g sat. fat), 46 mg chol., 142 mg sodium, 22 g carbo., 1 g fiber, 3 g pro. Daily values: 5% vit. A, 0% vit. C, 1% calcium, 7% iron

---

Tomato-Cheese Spread Appetizer

Pack the cheese mixture into a small crock and decorate the top of the cheese with additional onion slices and a snip of dried tomato. Present it with a plastic bag of toasted bread rounds or include some purchased crackers or melba toast.

2 8-ounce packages cream cheese, softened
2 tablespoons milk
2 teaspoons Worcestershire sauce
¼ cup oil-packed dried tomatoes, drained and finely chopped
¼ cup chopped pitted ripe olives
3 tablespoons thinly sliced green onions with tops
Toasted Bread Rounds

For spread, beat cream cheese in a large mixing bowl with an electric mixer until smooth. Beat in the milk and Worcestershire sauce until creamy. Stir in the tomatoes, olives, and onion until combined. Store, tightly covered, in the refrigerator up to 5 days. Serve the spread with Toasted Bread Rounds. Makes 2½ cups spread.

TOASTED BREAD ROUNDS: Cut one 16-ounce loaf baguette-style French bread into about forty ¼-inch-thick slices. Place slices in a single layer on baking sheets. Bake in a 400° oven about 8 minutes or until crisp and light brown, turning once halfway through baking. Cool. Store in a tightly covered container at room temperature.

Nutrition facts per tablespoon with bread: 74 cal., 5 g total fat (3 g sat. fat), 13 mg chol., 111 mg sodium, 6 g carbo., 0 g fiber, 2 g pro. Daily values: 5% vit. A, 2% vit. C, 1% calcium, 2% iron

141

Cranberry Brioche

Gingerbread Scone Mix

Lemon Curd

blender until mixture resembles coarse crumbs. Store in an airtight container up to 6 weeks at room temperature or up to 6 months in the freezer.

For each gift, measure about 1¾ cups mixture into a container. Include a recipe for Gingerbread Scones with each gift. Makes 3 gifts.

GINGERBREAD SCONES: Place gingerbread mix in a medium bowl. Make a well in center of dry mixture. Combine 2 tablespoons milk, 1 tablespoon molasses, and 1 beaten egg; add to dry mixture. Stir just until moistened. Turn dough out onto lightly floured surface. Quickly knead dough by folding and pressing it gently for 10 to 12 strokes or until dough is nearly smooth. Pat or lightly roll dough into a 6-inch circle. Cut into 6 wedges. Place wedges 1 inch apart on an ungreased baking sheet. Brush with a little milk and sprinkle with coarse or granulated sugar. Bake in a 400° oven for 10 to 12 minutes or until bottoms are brown. Serve warm. Makes 6 scones.

Nutrition facts per scone (1/18 of recipe): 207 cal., 10 g total fat (3 g sat. fat), 36 mg chol., 213 mg sodium, 26 g carbo., 1 g fiber, 4 g pro. Daily values: 1% vit. A, 0% vit. C, 11% calcium, 11% iron

Gingerbread Scone Mix

Place the scone mix in a tightly covered container or a plastic bag and wrap it with colorful fabric. Tie the fabric with raffia and attach a new wooden spoon and a recipe card with directions for preparing the mix.

    3¾ cups all-purpose flour
     ½ cup packed brown sugar
     2 tablespoons baking powder
     2 teaspoons ground ginger
     1 teaspoon ground cinnamon
     ½ teaspoon salt
     ¼ teaspoon baking soda
     ¼ teaspoon ground cloves
     ¼ teaspoon ground nutmeg
     ¾ cup shortening

Combine flour, sugar, baking powder, ginger, cinnamon, salt, baking soda, cloves, and nutmeg in a large mixing bowl. Cut in shortening with a pastry

Lemon Curd

Accompany the Gingerbread Scone Mix with a jar of this lemon spread. It's similar in consistency and flavor to the lemon layer in a lemon meringue pie.

     1 cup sugar
    1½ teaspoons cornstarch
     ⅓ cup lemon juice
     ¼ cup butter, cut up
     3 beaten eggs
     4 teaspoons finely shredded
        lemon peel

Combine sugar, cornstarch, and lemon juice in a medium saucepan. Add butter. Cook and stir over medium

heat until thickened and bubbly. Cook and stir for 2 minutes more.

Stir about half of the mixture into beaten eggs. Return all to saucepan. Reduce heat; cook and stir 1 to 2 minutes more or until mixture begins to thicken. *Do not boil.* Strain to remove any egg particles. Gently stir lemon peel into hot mixture and pour into small jars. Cool. Cover and refrigerate up to 1 month. Makes 1¾ cups spread.

Nutrition facts per tablespoon: 51 cal., 2 g total fat (1 g sat. fat), 27 mg chol., 23 mg sodium, 8 g carbo., 0 g fiber, 1 g pro. Daily values: 2% vit. A, 3% vit. C, 0% calcium, 0% iron

Anise Candy Crystals

Fill a candy jar or an antique container with these colorful, licorice-flavored candy pieces.

     2 cups sugar
     ½ cup light-colored corn syrup
     ½ cup water
     ½ teaspoon oil of anise
        Several drops red food coloring

Line an 8×8×2-inch baking pan with foil, extending the foil up the sides of the pan. Lightly butter the bottom of the foil-lined pan; set aside.

Stir together sugar, corn syrup, and water in a medium saucepan. Cook and stir over medium-high heat until mixture boils, stirring to dissolve the sugar. Clip a candy thermometer to side of the pan. Reduce heat to medium; continue boiling at a moderate, steady rate, stirring occasionally, until thermometer registers 290°, the soft-crack stage (about 25 minutes). Remove pan from heat; remove thermometer.

When boiling stops, quickly stir in the oil of anise and red food coloring and pour into the prepared pan. Let stand 5 to 10 minutes or until a film forms over the surface of the candy. Using a broad spatula or pancake turner, begin marking candy by pressing a line across surface ¾ inch from edge of pan. Do not break film on surface. Repeat along other 3 sides of pan, intersecting lines at corners to form squares. (If lines do not remain in candy, it is not yet cool enough to mark.) Continue marking lines along all sides ¾ inch apart, until you reach the center. Repeat scoring. Cool completely. **Use foil to lift candy** out of pan; remove foil from back and break candy into square pieces, tapping on back with a knife blade. Store in a jar. Makes about 100 pieces (18 ounces).

Nutrition facts per piece: 20 cal., 0 g total fat (0 g sat. fat), 0 mg chol., 1 mg sodium, 5 g carbo., 0 g fiber, 0 g pro. Daily values: 0% vit. A, 0% vit. C, 0% calcium, 0% iron

Nut Bread

Wrap the loaf in plastic wrap and place it in a ceramic container. Tie it up with wide organdy ribbon and a few small ornaments for a festive presentation.

  3 cups all-purpose flour
  1 cup sugar
  1 tablespoon baking powder
  ½ teaspoon salt
  ¼ teaspoon baking soda
  1 beaten egg
  1⅔ cups milk
  ¼ cup cooking oil
  ¾ cup chopped almonds, pecans, or walnuts

Grease bottom and ½ inch up sides of a 9×5×3-inch loaf pan; set aside.

Stir together flour, sugar, baking powder, salt, and soda. Make well in center; set aside. Combine egg, milk, and oil in a bowl. Add egg mixture all at once to flour mixture. Stir just until moistened (batter should be lumpy). Fold in nuts. Spoon into prepared pan. **Bake in a 350° oven** for 1 to 1¼ hours or until a wooden toothpick inserted in center comes out clean. Cool in pan on a wire rack 10 minutes. Remove loaf from pan. Cool completely on a wire rack. Wrap and store overnight before slicing. Makes 1 loaf (18 servings).

Nutrition facts per serving: 187 cal., 7 g total fat (1 g sat. fat), 14 mg chol., 153 mg sodium, 28 g carbo., 1 g fiber, 4 g pro. Daily values: 1% vit. A, 0% vit. C, 7% calcium, 7% iron

Nut Bread

143

For the true book lover, assemble a few treats to enhance his or her enjoyment of a favorite pastime. Box up some bookmarks, highlighters, a protective book cover, and a small dictionary to keep handy by the bed. Book plates and an embossing tool let your friend give favorite books a personal stamp. A small portable reading light makes reading in bed easy.

In a Twinkling: Gifts

▲ If the song your favorite handyperson most often sings is "If I Had a Hammer," answer the plea with a backup tool kit to store in the kitchen or den. Fill a rectangular plastic basket with a small hammer, various screwdrivers (Phillips, slot, large and small), a tape measure, and pliers, both needle-nose and plain. Tools will always be handy when they're needed.

◄ Give a relaxing night at the movies with all the comforts of home: package a tub of microwaveable popcorn with a videotape of a favorite movie and perhaps a certificate for a movie rental. Some candy, bottles of soda, and a copy of a comprehensive movie guide complete the gift.

 For friends or family members who usually eat lunch at their desks, make the experience more civilized with a lunch-for-one set that fits into a desk drawer. Camp flatware, a microwave-safe plate, mini salt and pepper shakers, and a place mat and napkins can all be stored in a small plastic box, along with a small bottle of dishwashing liquid for cleanup.

145

▲ If someone on your gift list is likely to make (again) that most common New Year's resolution, help him or her put a best foot forward with a "bouquet" of athletic socks, wrist bands, wrist or ankle weights, shoelaces, and a certificate for a visit to a local health club for a class or fitness evaluation.

▶

For the tiny tots on your list, make bath time a rub-a-dub good time with a net bag full of bubble bath, floating toys, a spout protector (shaped like a friendly animal), and children's soap in fun shapes.

Why not start a new tradition this year and set aside an afternoon for family creativity? A few hours spent baking or crafting can be lots of fun—and kids will take great pride in being able to say "I made it myself" when they present gifts to neighbors, teachers, or friends. Crafts or cooking can form the centerpiece of a holiday party, too. Decorating gingerbread house fronts like those on *pages 94–97* makes a good party project for pre-teens or teens. Bake the house fronts ahead of time and have an assortment of candies and plenty of royal icing on hand for trimming the houses. In case first-time decorators feel unsure about where to start, have a few illustrations or photos of gingerbread houses available to give them some ideas. The holidays are also an excellent opportunity to teach "an attitude of gratitude." To underscore the message that receiving a gift calls for a response, help kids make their own note cards. It's a great way to turn writing thank-you notes into an afternoon of crafting fun.

STUFF

Get your kids involved in crafting for the holidays with cards and gifts for teachers, friends, or siblings.

crafts *for kids*

It's never too early for children to learn good manners, and writing thank-you notes after the holidays is a good place to start. Turn the task into a craft with rubber stamps, paper punches, and blank card stock. For tips on helping kids with note-writing, see page 150.

Mittens Card

here's how...

1 Stamp two mittens in black ink on the red card stock or heavy paper. Cut them out.

2 Position the right mitten on the card to determine where to glue one end of the yarn. Remove the mitten and glue the yarn in place. Glue the mitten over the end of the yarn.

Glue two foam dots to the wrong side of the left mitten, and glue the foam dots to the card.

4 Stamp "Thanks" in red ink on the card.

Snowflake Card

here's how...

Punch snowflakes out of the blue paper and glue them randomly to the front of the card.

2 Using the blue stamp pad, stamp the word "Thanks" on the card and stamp small snowflakes randomly around it.

3 Use the glue marker to apply a coat of glue to the punched blue snowflakes, then sprinkle glitter over them.

4 Punch one snowflake out of the front of the card.

Tips for writing thank-you notes

 Two things are true throughout the known world: Kids love to get presents and hate to write thank-you notes. Convincing them to write often becomes a little easier when you remind them that someone took the time to find a gift, wrap or package it, and ship or deliver it. In return, all your child has to do is write a thoughtful note.

be prepared

Before the gifts even arrive, have your children put paper, pen, and postage at the ready. And when they do sit down to write, have them start with the right frame of mind: Instill the idea of thanking the person for the thought as much as for the gift.

write promptly

The sooner the better. A lull in activities on Christmas afternoon? Sit down and start writing! No more than a week should elapse from the receipt of the gift to the mailing of a note.

How young to start? As soon as children can appreciate the fact that someone has sent them a gift, they should participate in writing a thank-you note.

Before a child can write, a parent putting pen to paper for her should do so in the child's voice. Begin the note with, "Emily has asked me to write you," then continue with the child's sentiments about the gift.

mention the gift

Etiquette experts may differ on whether to start with the words "thank you," but all agree that you should mention the gift. Sounds obvious, but many a clever child has scribbled a string of "Thank you for the lovely Christmas present" form letters, signed his or her name, and gotten through the task in record time. Someone took the time to choose and send the gift; encourage your child to consider that effort and to take the time to respond with appropriate consideration.

Thank you first? Starting with the words "thank you" is considered trite by some etiquette experts. Not sending a note is, however, a worse breach of etiquette. So encourage your child to be creative, but don't discourage him from writing if all that comes from the pen is "Thank you for...."

make a connection with the gift

One excuse of thank-you note procrastinators is "I don't know what to say." Here's a list of questions to get started:

What do you like most about the gift? Is the color or design special or a favorite?

"Green is my favorite color, so I especially like the gloves you sent."

Were you really hoping to get this item or was it a delightful surprise?

"I was really hoping to get new in-line skates for Christmas, and I'm so glad to get them from you."

Will you be able to use the present right away or will you have to wait?

"As soon as spring comes, I'll be on the court to use the tennis racquet you sent."

Does this gift start, add to, or complete a set of collectibles?

"The Beanie Babies you chose complete my set!"

How will you use the gift? This is especially important for money gifts.

"Your generous gift will help me get new software for my computer."

and with the sender

Again, avoid stale or overused expressions. "How are you?" gets the job done but doesn't convey any personal thought. What does your child know of the gift giver's hobbies, travel plans, work, or home life? If Uncle Bob loves cars or Aunt Sue is planning a trip to Europe, encourage your child to mention those things in the note.

share news

Thank-you notes are in order mostly when someone is unable to be with your family for the holiday. These faraway relatives and friends will enjoy a brief update on family and personal activities.

every gift deserves a thank you

Even those gifts that miss the mark. You may be wondering what in the world Aunt Bernice was thinking when she bought your child that sweater, but she still deserves to be thanked for taking the time to select and send something. It's an opportunity to teach tact. In these situations, your child should, of course, mention the gift; but putting the emphasis on the thought behind it erases the need to heap false praise on an item.

Menorah Sweatshirt

SHOPPING LIST:
sweatshirt
tracing paper
heat transfer pencil
iron
cardboard to fit the shirt
paintbrush
fabric paints: pearlized
    gold, gold glitter,
    other colors as desired

Holiday fun includes wearing special clothes. Paint a sweatshirt for your own child or grandchild, or help an older child make one for a younger brother or sister.

here's how...

1 Prewash and dry your sweatshirt.

4 Paint the menorah with pearlized gold paint; after the paint dries, apply a coat of gold glitter over the pearlized paint. Referring to the photo for guidance, paint the candles with different colors of paint, rinsing the brush carefully between colors.

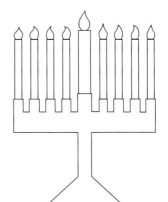

5 For the flames, dab orange and yellow paint at the top of each candle, then blend with a toothpick. Allow the shirt to dry flat for 24 hours.

2 Enlarge the pattern, *above right,* on a copy machine until it is the desired size. Trace the design onto a sheet of tracing paper using the heat transfer pencil, and then iron it onto the front of the sweatshirt (the design will be reversed when you transfer it). Note: The heat transfer pencil is permanent.

6 Turn the sweatshirt inside out and heat-set with an iron for 60 seconds.

7 Wait 72 hours before first laundering the sweatshirt. When laundering, turn the sweatshirt inside out and use warm water on a gentle cycle. Place it flat or hang it on a clothesline to dry.

151

3 Slip the cardboard inside the sweatshirt. (Don't use a wax-covered shirt board because the heat of the iron will melt the wax.) Smooth the design area of the sweatshirt over the cardboard.

Here's My Heart

❧Lightweight earrings made from air-drying modeling compound make good gifts for teachers. Younger children will need an adult to attach the jewelry parts.

From a crafts store:
- white air-drying modeling compound (not modeling clay)
- two ¾-inch eye pins
- fish-hook wires or ear wires for pierced earrings
- needle-nose pliers
- acrylic paints: red, gold glitter
- foam paintbrush
- white crafts glue

1 Shape the modeling compound into free-form heart shapes or other shapes.

2

2 Using the needle-nose pliers, bend the straight end of each eye pin into a hook. Insert the hook into the center top of the earring; the hook will keep the eye pin from sliding out after the modeling compound dries. (Make sure the eye pin doesn't show

through the surface of the shape.) Add a drop of white crafts glue where the pin enters the modeling compound to help secure it.

3 Let the modeling compound air-dry for several days. Apply two coats of red acrylic paint, letting the paint dry between coats. Apply a thin coat of gold glitter paint over the red.

4 Attach the fish-hook wires or ear wires to the eye pins, pinching the loops closed with the needle-nose pliers.

Mini-Treasure Chests

153

ᘛ These boxes are perfect for presenting tiny tokens to teachers and friends. Start with nested papier-mâché boxes from a crafts store, or recycle gift boxes to make these little containers. These are decorated with tree-shaped pasta, but if you can't find this at your grocery store, substitute bow-tie pasta or tiny stars. Tuck a small gift into each box—candy, a lapel pin, or a pair of earrings. The boxes themselves are a gift, too, handy for storing little treasures.

1 Using the foam paintbrush, apply two coats of red, green, or white paint to each box, letting the paint dry completely between coats.

2 Glue the pasta to the box top as shown. Let the glue dry.

3 Apply a light coat of gold glitter paint to the entire box, including the pasta.

SHOPPING LIST

From a crafts store:
  small papier-mâché
    boxes in
    graduated sizes
  acrylic paints: red,
    green, white, gold glitter
  foam paintbrush
  white crafts glue

From a grocery store:
  pasta shaped like
    Christmas trees

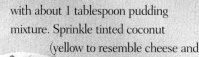
Cookie "Tostadas"

with about 1 tablespoon pudding mixture. Sprinkle tinted coconut (yellow to resemble cheese and green to resemble lettuce), chocolate pieces, and cherries on top to resemble "tostadas." Makes 14 to 16 cookies.

*Note: To make yellow- and green-tinted coconut, combine half of the coconut and a few drops of yellow food coloring in a small bowl. Mix until all coconut is colored. Repeat with remaining coconut and green food coloring.

Nutrition facts per cookie: 113 cal., 5 g total fat (2 g sat. fat), 3 mg chol., 85 mg sodium, 16 g carbo., 0 g fiber, 1 g pro. Daily values: 0% vit. A, 0% vit. C, 1% calcium, 2% iron

Cookie "Tostadas"

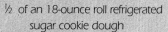

½ of an 18-ounce roll refrigerated sugar cookie dough
1 3.5-ounce container refrigerated chocolate pudding
¼ of an 8-ounce container frozen whipped dessert topping, thawed
¼ cup yellow- and green-tinted coconut*
Miniature semisweet chocolate pieces and chopped red maraschino or candied red cherries

Wrap and freeze the half-roll of cookie dough for 30 minutes or until firm (refrigerate remaining half-roll for another use). Using a serrated knife, cut frozen dough into ¼-inch-thick slices. Place on ungreased cookie sheets.

Bake in a 350° oven for 8 to 10 minutes or until set around the edges. Cool on cookie sheet for 1 minute. Remove cookies and cool completely on a wire rack.

Just before serving, fold together the pudding and whipped topping in a small mixing bowl. Top each cookie

Christmas Tree Cookie Treats

Peanut-flavored cookies in the shape of Christmas trees are especially fun to decorate with assorted candies and colored frosting.

½ cup peanut butter
¼ cup shortening
¼ cup butter, softened
½ cup granulated sugar
½ cup packed brown sugar
½ teaspoon baking powder
½ teaspoon baking soda
1 egg
1 teaspoon vanilla
1⅓ cups all-purpose flour
Flat wooden sticks
Purchased frosting and small candy pieces (optional)

Grease tree-shaped aluminum cookie treat pans. Set aside.

Beat peanut butter, shortening, and butter in a large mixing bowl with an electric mixer on medium to high speed for 30 seconds. Add granulated sugar, brown sugar, baking powder, and baking soda; beat until combined. Beat in egg and vanilla until combined. Beat in as much of the flour as you can with the mixer. Stir in any remaining flour with a wooden spoon. If necessary, cover and chill dough until easy to handle.

Pat 1 rounded tablespoon of dough into each tree shape in prepared pan. Place a flat wooden stick about 1 inch into each tree shape on top of dough. Pat 1 rounded tablespoon of dough on top of stick.

Bake in a 350° oven for 12 minutes or until edges are lightly browned. Let cool for 10 minutes in pan on a wire rack. Remove cookies from pan; cool completely on rack. Decorate with frosting and small colored candies, if desired. Makes about 15 cookies.

Nutrition facts per cookie: 198 cal., 11 g total fat (4 g sat. fat), 22 mg chol., 132 mg sodium, 22 g carbo., 1 g fiber, 4 g pro. Daily values: 3% vit. A, 0% vit. C, 1% calcium, 5% iron

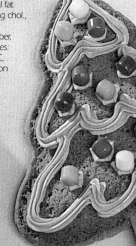

Christmas Tree Cookie Treats

kids *in the* kitchen

Polka-Dotted Cookies

Buttery sugar cookies studded with colorful candy-coated pieces are a playful version of the classic Mexican Wedding Cake or Sandies cookie recipes.

  1 cup butter, softened
  ⅓ cup granulated sugar
  1 tablespoon milk
  1 teaspoon vanilla
  2¼ cups all-purpose flour
  ½ cup miniature candy-coated
      semisweet or milk
      chocolate pieces
      Red- and/or green-colored
      sugar (optional)
  1 cup sifted chocolate-flavored
      powdered sugar

Beat butter in a large mixing bowl with an electric mixer on medium to high speed for 30 seconds. Add granulated sugar; beat until combined, scraping sides of bowl occasionally. Beat in milk and vanilla until combined. Beat in as much of the flour as you can with the mixer. Stir in any remaining flour and the miniature chocolate pieces with a wooden spoon.

Shape dough into 1-inch balls. Place the balls about 1 inch apart on an ungreased cookie sheet. (If desired, dip tops of cookies in red- or green-colored sugar before baking.)

Bake in a 325° oven for 18 to 20 minutes or until bottoms are lightly browned. Transfer cookies to a wire rack and let cool. For cookies not dipped in colored sugar, gently shake cooled cookies in a plastic bag with the chocolate powdered sugar. Makes about 48 cookies.

Nutrition facts per cookie: 75 cal., 4 g total fat (2 g sat. fat), 10 mg chol., 39 mg sodium, 9 g carbo., 0 g fiber, 1 g pro. Daily values: 3% vit. A, 0% vit. C, 0% calcium, 1% iron

No-Measure Bars

These rich, chunky bar cookies are quick to make and simple enough for young children to help assemble.

  ½ stick butter or margarine
      (¼ cup)
  15 to 18 graham cracker squares
  1 12-ounce package semisweet
      chocolate pieces
  1 3½-ounce can flaked coconut
  1 2-ounce package chopped
      walnuts (½ cup)
  1 14-ounce can sweetened
      condensed milk

Line a 13×9×2-inch baking pan with foil, extending foil over edges of pan. Place butter in pan. With adult help, heat in a 350° oven about 1 minute or until butter melts.

Place graham cracker squares in butter in pan, breaking them, if necessary, to cover bottom of pan. Layer, in order, the chocolate pieces, coconut, and walnuts. Pour sweetened condensed milk evenly over all.

Bake in a 350° oven for 25 to 30 minutes. Cool. Lift foil and cookies from baking pan. Cut into squares or bars. Makes 24 to 36 cookies.

Nutrition facts per cookie: 194 cal., 11 g total fat (2 g sat. fat), 11 mg chol., 77 mg sodium, 24 g carbo., 0 g fiber, 3 g pro. Daily values: 3% vit. A, 0% vit. C, 4% calcium, 4% iron

No-Measure Bars

Even Santa has to pack smart if he expects gifts to arrive in fine fashion. After all, there are a few bumps in the road from the North Pole—or your house—to the homes of friends and family.

sending
your best

When you're sending handmade gifts, take a little extra care to ensure the items you worked so hard to create arrive at the homes of friends and relatives safely and on time:

use a good shipping box.

Don't skimp on size or sturdiness. A store gift box won't do; corrugated cardboard is a necessity. Shipping companies and stores sell heavy-duty boxes at reasonable prices; many department stores sell them during the holidays, too. And use wide package tape to ensure the box holds its shape while it's in transit.

if you're recycling an old
shipping box, remove old labels and cross through or cover old shipping information to prevent your package from getting misdirected.

so the cookie doesn't crumble

Keeping holiday treats intact in transit takes a little planning:
■ Bake cookies right before you're ready to send them so they'll be as fresh as possible. And ship them early in the week so they don't sit in a warehouse getting stale over the weekend.

■ Frost at your peril. Glazes that dry to a hard finish will hold up, but regular frosting will likely get mushed and sprinkles just fall off.

■ Within the box, wrap cookies individually or in back-to-back pairs to keep them from rubbing each other to crumbs.

■ Layer wrapped cookies by weight, putting the heaviest cookies on the bottom.

■ Use plastic- or foil-lined heavy boxes to hold the cookies. Slip a couple sheets of paper towels and waxed paper between layers of homemade cookies and treats to protect them. Wrap the layers together, protecting the edges from the side of the containers, then wrap the box snugly in bubble wrap or surround it in "peanuts" so it floats in the shipping box. You shouldn't feel anything shift when you shake the box.

use large, clearly marked labels.
Be sure to fill them out completely and accurately, including zip code and full street address information. To protect address information from rain and snow, cover the completed label with wide, clear shipping tape. (Put address information inside the package, too. If the address label gets damaged, the package can still be delivered or returned to you.)

package internal items separately.
Even the sturdiest items can dent or break when they bump against each other in the box, or they can damage more fragile items. Batteries left in electronics can jostle enough to do damage. Packaging items of like weight and durability together is the best solution. Package fragile items separately from each other and from other items.

use bubble wrap
or fluffy packing "peanuts" for most items. Crumpled paper compresses in shipping, making it less effective in protecting your gifts, so use paper only for light, but not fragile, items. The print from newspaper can smudge gift paper. If you want to use paper, use kraft paper or a similar product.

extra padding
is extra insurance for fragile items. Packing "peanuts" and sheets of bubble wrap are lightweight ways to protect breakables in shipping.

gift wrap
if you wish, but forgo the bow—it will likely get flattened in shipping. Instead, use a wide ribbon to crisscross the package, and hold the ends in place with a fancy sticker.

protect with insurance, too.
Most items make it to their destinations without incident, but some don't. Insure your package for its retail value. UPS automatically insures packages for up to $100, and you can buy more insurance if necessary. Keep the receipt with the tracking number so you can properly file a claim if needed.

ship early.
If your package is in the deluge crisscrossing the country in the days before Christmas, it's more likely to be lost or damaged—or delivered late.

credits & sources

pages 8–15: design, Aubrey Dunbar; photos, Peter Krumhardt

pages 16–19: concept, Kaye Lorraine; styling, Rebecca Jerdee; assistant stylist, Jenny Stoffel; photos, Peter Krumhardt

pages 20–21: design and styling, Rebecca Jerdee; assistant stylist, Jenny Stoffel; photos, Peter Krumhardt

pages 22–27: design, Nancy Wall Hopkins; photos, Hopkins Associates

pages 28–33: stylist, Jilann Severson; photos, Peter Krumhardt. Lights: GKI, available at major retail stores; clips and stakes: Santa's Best, available at major retail and craft stores.

pages 34–37: vine balls: to order, call Gardener's Supply, 800/863-1700; birdbath: to order, call Smith & Hawkin, 800/776-3336; geese: for the store nearest you, call The Rusted Garden, 800/247-4178; stylist, Wade Scherrer; photos, Peter Krumhardt; porch with bears: stylist, Rebecca Jerdee; photos, Tom McWilliam

page 38: produced by Michele Michaels; photograph of finished topiary, Bill Holt; step by step photos, Peter Krumhardt

page 39: design, Abby Ruoff; photos, William Stites; step by steps: styled by Jilann Severson; photos, Peter Krumhardt

pages 40–41: switchplates, Jilann Severson; curtain tiebacks, Dondra Green Parham; photo corsages, Aubrey Dunbar; photos, Peter Krumhardt; minitree, Peggy Johnston; photo, King Au

pages 42–45: magnolia wreath, lime and bay wreath produced by Michele Michaels; photos, Bill Holt; lemon leaf wreath and ivy wreath: design, Jim Williams; photos, Andy Lyons; kumquat wreath: design, Rebecca Jerdee; photos, Barbara Martin

pages 46–47: snowflake pillow: design and styling, Rebecca Jerdee; photos, Tom McWilliam; ivy, poinsettia pillows: design, Dondra G. Parham; photos, Perry Struse

pages 48–49: Joy to the World lamp: design, Jeni Hilpipre; photo, Jenifer Jordan; step by steps styled by Jilann Severson, photos by Peter Krumhardt; decoupage lampshade: design, Geri Wolfe Boesen; photo, Jenifer Jordan

pages 50–53: designers, Jim Williams, Sandi Guely; photos, King Au

pages 54–55: spicy balls and stars: design, Nancy Wall Hopkins; photos, Hopkins Associates; wire trees: design, Heidi T. King; photos, Peter Krumhardt; crackled ball ornaments: design, Nancy Worrell; photos, Peter Krumhardt

pages 56–57: milk carton candles: design, Peggy Johnston; main photo, Andy Lyons; how-to photos, Bryan McKay; appliqué candles: design, Heidi T. King; photos, Peter Krumhardt

pages 58–59: silvered candles, leaf candle, teacup candles: design and styling, Jilann Severson; photos, Peter Krumhardt; candle on sconce, Peggy Johnston; photo, King Au; candles in glassware, photo, Hopkins Associates

page 62: stylist, Jennifer Peterson; photos, Peter Krumhardt

page 65: photos, Mike Dieter

pages 68–74: stylist, Jennifer Peterson; photos, Peter Krumhardt

pages 76–81: boxwood tree: regional editor, Estelle Bond Guralnick; photos, D. Randolph Foulds; stacked buckets of fruit: design, Cort Schwanebeck; photo, Andy Lyons; paper lanterns: design, Rebecca Jerdee; photo, Tom McWilliam; platter: design, Jim Williams; photo, King Au; apples and roses: design, Vicki Ingham; photo, Peter Krumhardt

page 83: stylist, Jennifer Peterson; photos, Peter Krumhardt

page 84: photo, Colleen Duffley

page 85: stylist, Janet Pittman; photos, Scott Little

pages 87–89: stylist, Jennifer Peterson; photos, Peter Krumhardt

page 91: stylist, Jennifer Peterson; photos, Mike Dieter

page 92: stylist, A.J. Battalfarano; photos, Ilisa Katz

page 93: stylist, Jennifer Peterson; photos, Scott Little

pages 94–97: stylist, Jennifer Peterson; photos, Mike Dieter

pages 98–101: stylist, Jennifer Peterson; photos, Peter Krumhardt

pages 102–103: mix and match red and green: concept Jilann Severson; clip-on ornament and candle, cranberry bobeche, and New Year's setting: design, Peggy Johnston; photos, Peter Krumhardt; pear place card holder: Michele Michaels; photos, Bill Holt

pages 104–107: bistro tables, enclosed porch: stylist, Rebecca Jerdee; tabard-style slipcovers: design, Dondra Green Parham; photos, Peter Krumhardt

page 109: stylist, Janet Pittman; photos, Tommy Miyasaki

page 110: stylist, Jennifer Peterson; photos, Mike Dieter

page 112: stylist, Judy Vance; photos, Tony Glaser

page 113: stylist, Janet Pittman; photos, Jim Krantz

pages 114–115: stylist, Jennifer Peterson; photos, Doug Smith

page 116: stylist, Jennifer Peterson; photo, Peter Krumhardt

page 118: stylist, Jennifer Peterson; photo, Andy Lyons

page 119: stylist, Jennifer Peterson; photo, Peter Krumhardt

page 120: stylist, Lynn Blanchard; photo, Mike Dieter

page 121: stylist, Jennifer Peterson; photos, Peter Krumhardt

pages 124–27: painted vase: design, Heidi T. King; photo, Peter Krumhardt; pinecone topiaries: design, Geri Wolfe Boesen; photo, Hopkins Associates; wine cozies, etched-glass plate: design, Jeni Hilpipre, Lynne Pekarek; photos, Jenifer Jordan, step by steps Peter Krumhardt

pages 128–30: designs, Peggy Johnston; photos, Peter Krumhardt

pages 132–33: bayleaf and cinnamon stick packages: design, Jennifer Ruiter; photos, Andy Lyons; bells and ornaments, Dondra Green Parham; ribbon and silk ivy, Aubrey Dunbar; hair bows and shoestrings, Peggy Johnston; photos, Peter Krumhardt

pages 134–37: amaryllis produced by Craig Summers Black; photos, Peter Krumhardt; seedlings, Cort Schwanebeck, photo, Andy Lyons

page 138: stylist, Jennifer Peterson; photo, Peter Krumhardt

page 140: stylist, Lynn Blanchard; photos, Scott Little

pages 141–42: stylist, Lynn Blanchard; photos, Mike Dieter

page 143: stylist, Jennifer Peterson; photo, Peter Krumhardt

pages 144–45: concepts, Paula Marshall; stylist Jilann Severson; photos, Peter Krumhardt

page 146: photo, John Kane

pages 148–49: thank-you cards, Marj Huber; photos, Peter Krumhardt. To order stamps, ink pads, paper punches, and blank card stock by mail, contact Outstamping Designs in West Des Moines; call 515/277-5719 for prices and ordering information.

page 151: menorah sweatshirt design, Heidi Knecht; step by steps styled by Jilann Severson, photos, Peter Krumhardt

page 152: heart earrings: design, Pam Kvitne, photos, Peter Krumhardt

page 153: pasta boxes: design, Ariana Kvitne, Alex Kvitne, and Megan Spooner; photo Peter Krumhardt

pages 154–55: stylist, Jennifer Peterson; photos, Peter Krumhardt

index

index *continued*